THE STORY OF
THE GAA

Vincent McDonnell is from County Mayo and now lives near Newmarket, County Cork. In 1989 he won the GPA First Fiction Award, after being recommended by Graham Greene. He has published two other non-fiction works and five novels for children. The winner of numerous prizes, he has been writer in residence at many venues and has given workshops and readings all over Ireland.

By the same author

Michael Collins: Most Wanted Man
Titanic Tragedy

THE STORY OF
THE GAA

VINCENT McDONNELL

The Collins Press

FIRST PUBLISHED IN 2009 BY
The Collins Press
West Link Park
Doughcloyne
Wilton
Cork

A Cataloguing-in-Publication record is available for this book from the
British Library.

ISBN: 978-1905172962

Typesetting by The Collins Press
Typeset in Garamond Premier Pro 13 pt
Printed in the UK by Athenaeum Press Limited

This book has been printed on paper that is sourced and harvested from
sustainable forests and is FSC-accredited.

Cover photographs of the Sam Maguire and Liam McCarthy cups
courtesy of Inpho

Contents

Introduction	1
The GAA	4
History of Hurling	20
Hurling Greats	36
History of Football	48
Football Greats	61
Hurling and Football Greats	71
GAA Competitions in Hurling and Football	76
Camogie	83
Ladies' Gaelic Football	88
International Rules	92
Handball	96
Great GAA Families	99
Famous GAA Grounds	105
Famous GAA People	112
County Colours	120
Facts & Figures	122
All-Ireland Senior Hurling Winners	122
All-Ireland Minor Hurling Winners	126
All-Ireland Hurling Club Winners	129
Hurling Titles Held	131
All-Ireland Senior Football Winners	134
All-Ireland Minor Football Winners	138
All-Ireland Football Club Winners	141
Football Titles Held	143

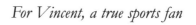

For Vincent, a true sports fan

INTRODUCTION

In Dublin city there is a small area of green grass. It measures 144 metres by 86 metres. Compared to Dublin's Phoenix Park, the largest enclosed urban park in Europe, this area of green grass is tiny. Yet it is the most famous piece of ground in all of Ireland. There is hardly a single Irish boy or girl who hasn't dreamed of one day running out onto that green turf with the roar of 80,000 people ringing in their ears.

That small area of ground is the centrepiece of a sports stadium named Croke Park, which is the headquarters of the largest sporting organisation in Ireland. This organisation is the Gaelic Athletic Association, or Cumann Lúthchleas Gael, better known to every schoolboy and girl as the GAA.

The GAA is more than simply a sporting organisation. Its presence is felt in every village and parish and town in Ireland. It is at the heart of rural and urban life. It has tens of thousands of members and over 2,000 clubs play games every week. Hurling, football and camogie are the most popular games, but the GAA also supports handball and many other cultural activities.

The most important days in the GAA calendar are those days when the finals of the major GAA competitions are held. These are the All-Ireland Football finals for men and women, the All-Ireland

Hurling and Camogie finals, and the All-Ireland Club finals in hurling and football.

On the days when these matches are played, up to 80,000 men, women and children pack Croke Park. Most support the teams contesting the finals. But other spectators come from every corner of Ireland to savour the atmosphere and enjoy the thrills and excitement of some of the finest field games in the world. Spectators come from abroad too, from Britain and America and other countries across the world. Millions of others watch the games on television and on the Internet, or listen to them on the radio.

Wherever Irish people gather the topic of football, hurling or camogie isn't far from their minds. One can hear them speak with awe of the great games and the great players. Names like Christy Ring, D. J. Carey and Angela Downey are still vividly spoken of by hurling and camogie fans. Football fans speak of Mick O'Connell, Pat Spillane, Sue Ramsbottom and Cora Staunton. Young people listen enthralled, and dream of one day playing in Croke Park and having people speak of them with similar awe.

But none of this could exist without the organisation known as the GAA, which was founded in 1884. Like the games itself, it has had a long, and at times, difficult history. But the vision and dream of Michael Cusack, who founded it, and of those who came after him, has seen it survive to become the most important sporting organisation in Ireland.

This is a history of how the GAA, from humble beginnings, became Ireland's premier sporting organisation. It is the story of a few men with vision who had a dream and set out to bring that dream to fruition. It is the story of those who came after them and continued their dream. It is also the story of how the GAA

Introduction

survived strife and war and violence and achieved the tremendous success and popularity it enjoys today.

But most of all it is the story of the sport and of those men and women who played, and still play the games. Some are heroes and heroines from the past who brought excitement and thrills and glory to the crowds who came to watch them. Others are the heroes and heroines of recent times whose exploits on the playing fields will be spoken about with awe by generations to come and whose names will never be forgotten.

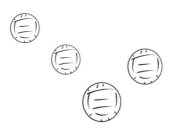

THE GAA

The Beginning

The GAA (Gaelic Athletic Association) or, in Irish, Cumann Lúthchleas Gael, was founded on Saturday 1 November 1884. At 3 p.m. on that Saturday, a group of men met in the billiard-room of Miss Hayes' Commercial Hotel in Thurles, County Tipperary. There were at least seven men present, though later reports state that the number was thirteen or fourteen.

The meeting was arranged by a Clareman, Michael Cusack. He was a teacher and a sportsman. When he moved from Clare to teach in Dublin, he tried to revive the game of hurling, which he had seen being played in his native county.

At this time there were two versions of hurling being played in Ireland. Cusack tried to combine these two different versions and set up the Dublin Hurling Club with this aim in mind. But disagreements arose between the players from both codes and the experiment failed.

Cusack then set up the Dublin Metropolitan Hurling Club, which played the version of the game known as hurling. This venture was a success in the Dublin area. Cusack then arranged a match between his club and a team from Killimor, in County

The GAA

Galway. Despite a dispute over scores, the game itself proved to be a success. A small seed had been sown.

Michael Cusack was a staunch Irishman. He believed that Ireland should preserve its own language, culture, traditions and native pastimes. It was to discuss how this might be achieved that the meeting was called in Thurles.

Along with an interest in hurling, Cusack was a fine athlete and a passionate supporter of athletics. From his involvement in this sport, he had become appalled at the state of Irish athletics. He was especially appalled at the neglect of what he regarded as native Irish pastimes.

His dream was to set up a body that would support and organise these national pastimes, especially running, jumping, throwing weights and wrestling. He also wanted the ordinary Irish person to be able to take part in athletic events and thus halt the continuing decline in native Irish pastimes and games.

Another important man present at the first meeting was Maurice Davin. He was from Carrick-on-Suir, County Tipperary, and was the most famous Irish athlete of his day. He, too, had ideas similar to Cusack's and was even more passionate about seeing the games of hurling and football revived. He was aware, like Cusack, that if no action was taken to revive hurling and football, they would soon disappear. Already they were losing ground to English games like rugby and cricket, both of which were becoming very popular in Ireland.

At that first meeting there was very little emphasis placed on the revival of Gaelic football or hurling. Most emphasis was placed on athletics. This seems strange today when the GAA is almost totally devoted to Gaelic football, hurling and camogie, (a form of hurling played by women). The GAA no longer plays any part in athletics in Ireland, and handball and international rules football are the only other sports the association supports.

In the years prior to the founding of the GAA, versions of hurling and football had been popular in many parts of the country. In rural areas they had been the main form of entertainment for the poorer people. Football and hurling matches between adjoining estates were usually organised by landlords. In these matches, the tenants and labourers from the estates would take part. For the players, and for those who came to watch the games, they were a form of recreation. For the landlords and those who were wealthy, they offered an opportunity for gambling, which was very popular among rich people at that time. Yet at the time the GAA was formed in 1884, both hurling and football were in serious decline, and had been for some time.

Hurling and Football in Decline

The decline in the playing of football and hurling in the 1800s had many reasons. Firstly, in 1798, there had been a rebellion in Ireland, organised by a group known as the United Irishmen. Ireland at this time was ruled from Britain and the United Irishmen wanted Ireland to be free from British rule.

Some tenant farmers and labourers took part in the rebellion. Afterwards, this led to strains between landlords and their tenants and labourers. As a result, landlords ceased to organise football and hurling matches between their estates. The authorities that governed the country also feared that crowds attending matches might use such gatherings to plan further rebellions. In many areas they forbade the people to gather. In other areas local officials, who were responsible for law and order, forbade the playing of matches.

At the beginning of the 1800s there was also great poverty in Ireland. One of the reasons for this was that Ireland had been under British rule for almost 700 years. Down through the centuries there had been many rebellions, like that of 1798, to try and drive the British out of Ireland. All had failed. As a result of these rebellions the British had suppressed the Irish people.

Not only were they forbidden schooling and to practise their religion, but they were not allowed to own land. The native Irish landowners had been hunted off their land, which had then been given to settlers from England and Scotland. This meant that many native Irish people were now forced to work as labourers or servants on the estates of these settlers or landlords. Other native Irish people rented farms from the landlords at very high rents. Most of the land was used for growing crops like grain that could be sold to obtain money to pay the rents. What was left over was used for growing potatoes for food.

The population had increased dramatically in the previous centuries, especially in rural Ireland. This meant that the already small farms had to be divided still further. Large families now struggled to eke out a living on small patches of land. Because of the need to grow crops to pay the ever-increasing rents, they were almost wholly dependant on the potato for food. This situation was worst among labourers. They were the poorest of the poor, and mostly lived in mud cabins virtually on the verge of starvation.

Famine was common, though it was usually restricted to small areas at any one time. But in 1845 there was widespread famine in Ireland. Thousands of people died of starvation and disease while thousands more emigrated. In the years 1845 to 1848 it's estimated that over a million Irish people died or left Ireland.

A sense of despair settled over the country. In the midst of such suffering, games of football and hurling seemed of little importance. In some areas so many people had died or emigrated that there were simply not enough men to form a team. By 1884, just forty years after the famine, when Michael Cusack and his supporters met to set up the GAA, both hurling and football were in real danger of extinction.

But while these Irish games had almost disappeared, English games like cricket and rugby were widely played. These were played and supported by those people from England who were in Ireland as government administrators. Cricket was also played by English soldiers who were garrisoned in the country. Indeed, by 1884 there were cricket clubs in almost every large town. Those from the Irish middle class – doctors, lawyers, teachers, shopkeepers and business people – also supported these games. They considered the almost extinct native Irish games as being suitable only for peasants.

These poorer people, or peasants, were also prevented from taking part in athletic events, which were organised in Ireland by the same body that controlled athletics in England. This was the Amateur Athletic Association (AAA). It considered that athletics were only suitable for gentlemen.

Michael Cusack was determined to do something about this situation. He realised that if those poorer Irish people were to have the opportunity to take part in athletic events, then they would have to form their own athletic body. Thus he called the meeting in Thurles where the GAA was founded on that Saturday in November 1884. In the beginning, Cusack and Davin saw the GAA's main focus as that of organising Irish athletics. Thus the name chosen for the new organisation was the Gaelic Athletic Association.

Neither Cusack nor Davin, nor the other men who met that Saturday, could ever have imagined how important football and hurling were to become for the GAA. Nor could they have imagined that within a few short years the emphasis on athletics would wane and that a day would come when the GAA would play no part in athletics in Ireland.

The Early Years

It was a very modest beginning for what was to become the most important and popular sporting organisation ever set up in Ireland. At that first meeting, Maurice Davin was elected President of the GAA while Michael Cusack became one of its secretaries. It was suggested at that first meeting that the newly formed organisation should invite Archbishop Croke of Cashel, Charles Stewart Parnell, leader of the Irish Parliamentary Party, (IPP) and Michael Davitt, founder of the Land League, to be patrons. While the latter two played only minor parts in the future of the GAA, Archbishop Croke became one of its most fervent and famous supporters. A statue in his honour was later erected in Thurles, but the greatest honour bestowed on him was the naming of the GAA's main stadium, Croke Park, after him.

The GAA was founded at a turbulent time in Ireland. The Famine was still a recent memory and an even more recent memory was the Fenian rebellion of 1869. It had been organised by men who had formed a secret society, the Irish Republican Brotherhood (IRB). The rising had failed but the IRB had remained in existence. Its aim was to win Ireland her freedom from English rule. They wanted Ireland to have its own parliament in Dublin, which would not be subject to the King of England.

At this time there was no Irish parliament. Those who were elected in Ireland had to sit in the London parliament. The Irish Parliamentary Party was the largest party in Ireland. It was led by Charles Stewart Parnell. Its aim was to obtain Home Rule for Ireland. It, too, wanted a parliament sitting in Dublin but this would remain subject to the King of England.

Both sides were always seeking ways of furthering their cause. So it is no surprise that both sides saw the GAA as a possible means of helping them to achieve their aims. In fact the desire of men within the IRB of using the GAA in this way almost led to the later failure of the organisation.

Though a staunch nationalist and a Fenian, Cusack intended that the GAA be a non-political organisation. Its aims were to further the needs of Irish athletes and to bring a sense of pride in being Irish. He was determined from the start not to allow the organisation to become involved in politics.

But Cusack was a strong-willed man who was easily roused to anger. This led him to make many enemies. He quarrelled with the members of the newly found GAA and within two years of the Thurles meeting he was dismissed. Afterwards, he played no part in the organisation. But such was the popularity of the athletic meetings organised by the GAA, and especially the football and hurling matches, that the organisation survived.

The GAA was founded at a time when nationalist feelings in Ireland were high. Michael Davitt had recently founded the Land League whose aim was to fight for tenant farmers' rights. People were beginning to have a sense of pride in being Irish, and there was a growing interest in Irish traditions and language, so much so that Douglas Hyde soon founded the Gaelic League with the intention of reviving and encouraging the Irish language. So if there was an ideal time to found an organisation to support Irish games and pastimes, this surely was it.

Success came quickly to the GAA. Within weeks of its founding it organised an athletic meeting in County Cork. In 1885 it organised a hurling match in County Galway, where hurling was still being played. A few months later, a football match under newly drawn up GAA rules was played in Kilkenny. By the end of the year athletic meetings were being held all over the country, though as yet football and hurling matches, if played at these events, were only of secondary importance.

By 1886 the first games featuring teams from different counties began to take place. Large crowds attended these games and also attended the athletic meetings. At a meeting in Tralee, County Kerry, a crowd of over 15,000 attended. At a time when public transport was almost non-existent and before the era of the motor-car, this was an extraordinary attendance.

The All-Ireland Football and Hurling Championships

In fact the GAA had become so strong and popular by 1887, a mere three years after its founding, that the first All-Ireland Football and Hurling championships were held. These involved club teams from each county rather than the county teams we know so well today. Nine counties took part in the football competition and five in the hurling. It was a small beginning but like the beginning of the GAA itself, the All-Ireland championships were destined to become the most important sporting events in the whole country, a position they still hold today.

The first All-Ireland Football champions were Limerick. Their club team, Commercials, beat Dundalk Young Irelands from Louth by 1-4 to 0-3. The game took place on 29 April 1888 at Clonskeagh, Dublin. In hurling, Thurles from Tipperary beat Meelick from Galway 1-1 to 0-0. This game was played on 1 April 1888 at Hoare's Field, in Birr, County Offaly. It was a small beginning but just like a mighty oak tree grows from a tiny acorn, so the GAA grew from that small beginning to become the largest and most popular sporting organisation Ireland has ever seen.

One of the main reasons for the success of the GAA was that it was based around the local parish right from the beginning. Teams from the smallest villages to the largest towns gave their area a focus where in most cases none existed before that. Only players from the parish were allowed to play on the parish team and this created a fierce pride in the locality. Local people had a reason to be proud of their village or town when the local team won a match.

This forming of teams in each parish created a ferocious rivalry between local parishes, a rivalry which exists to this very day and which has been carried over into inter-county contests. In fact some of the greatest and most memorable games have been those between adjoining rival parishes or counties.

It is a credit to the GAA and its supporters that this rivalry, while intense on the field and among rival supporters, has rarely boiled over into violence. Indeed, it is a great hallmark of the GAA to see fervent groups of rival supporters exchanging good-hearted banter as they make their way to a stadium.

Afterwards, no matter which team has won, those same rival supporters often get together to discuss the match and to argue the merits of players and officials and scores and what might have been. This is the heartbeat of the GAA and while this rivalry and pride continues in this good-natured way, the GAA will continue to thrive.

Troubled Times

Although the GAA had great success at the beginning, its very existence was soon threatened. Threats came from many quarters. One threat was the dismissal of Cusack. Others came from those groups who saw the GAA as a means of furthering their political aims. The main groups were the Parnellites, who sought Home Rule through peaceful means, and the Fenians and the secret Irish Republican Brotherhood (IRB) who both wished to win Ireland her freedom through physical force.

Those in authority who saw the GAA as a threat to stability in Ireland also sought to undermine the organisation and accused it of being politically motivated. When a scandal erupted around the life of Charles Stewart Parnell it caused his political party to split in two. Many of those in the party were also involved in the GAA and the Parnell split almost led to a split in the GAA. Had a split occurred, it might have destroyed the organisation.

Most GAA members supported Parnell and the problem created by the Parnell split was only resolved when Parnell died and his party reunited. But a threat still remained from those in the IRB and indeed they did take control of the GAA for a time. But despite this and financial problems, the organisation survived.

There was also opposition to the GAA from those athletes who were in the AAA and also from others who disliked Cusack. In 1885 they formed the Irish Amateur Athletic Association (IAAA), which survived for forty years. Yet despite these early setbacks the GAA gained momentum and by 1887, an astonishing 600 clubs had been set up. But more troubled times lay ahead.

In 1916, the Easter Rising took place in Ireland. Afterwards a guerrilla war, known as the War of Independence began in Ireland. The guerrillas who fought this war, and who later became known as the Irish Republican Army (IRA), were supported by the political party Sinn Féin. Many members and supporters of Sinn Féin were also involved in the GAA. This again caused problems for the organisation, which was once more accused of being involved in politics. But such was the strength of the GAA that it survived.

The years 1916 to 1923 were violent years in Ireland. Yet despite the violence matches were played and the All-Ireland championships continued, even though in some years the actual finals were not played until the following years.

Then, on Sunday 21 November 1920, events occurred in Dublin, which make that day the darkest in the GAA's history. Even today that day is still better known as 'Bloody Sunday'. On that morning, IRA men acting on the orders of Michael Collins, the director of the guerrilla war, killed over a dozen British spies in Dublin.

The GAA

On that fateful day, a football match between Dublin and Tipperary was being played in Croke Park. In retaliation for the killing of the British spies, the Black and Tans and Auxies, which were part of the British armed forces in Ireland, burst into Croke Park, opened fire on the players and crowd and killed fourteen people. Among the dead was Tipperary footballer, Michael Hogan. Today his death is fittingly marked by the Hogan Stand in Croke Park, which is named in his memory.

In 1921, Sinn Féin, the largest political party in Ireland, signed a treaty with the British government. Under this treaty, twenty-six counties were to become known as the Free State. The remaining six became known as Northern Ireland.

There were many who fought in the War of Independence who did not agree with this treaty. This led to civil war in Ireland. Again this caused problems for the GAA. Now GAA supporters fought on opposite sides in the conflict and there was much bitterness between them.

In 1923 the Civil War ended, yet the bitterness remained. The GAA now played a significant part in easing this bitterness. Men who had fought on opposing sides in the Civil War now joined together again to play hurling and football for their parishes and counties. The pride they had in their parishes and counties and in representing them overcame any hatred they might have held toward each other.

Over the coming years there were many setbacks for the GAA. Kerry withdrew from the championship in 1935 because of the way Republican prisoners were being treated by the Irish government. In Northern Ireland the GAA had to overcome major opposition from the Protestant and Loyalist government and population. Yet it did so admirably, and hurling and football grew in strength in the province. In recent times teams from Northern Ireland have featured strongly in the championship, especially in football, and have won numerous All-Ireland titles.

The Controversial Rules

Despite its success, the GAA has had to face criticism on a number of fronts. One of these criticisms concerned Rule 27, better known as The Ban. When the GAA was founded its aim was to promote Irish pastimes, which were being threatened by 'foreign' ones, that is, games brought to Ireland from England. These games were primarily soccer, rugby and cricket.

From time to time in the early years, those who took part in GAA games were forbidden to take part in, or attend, these 'foreign' games. This was intended to help the survival of the Irish pastimes. Then from 1902 on this rule was rigidly enforced. In 1938 this led to Douglas Hyde, who was then President of Ireland, being removed as a patron of the association because as President he had attended a soccer match. After much heated debate, in 1971, at a GAA congress in Belfast, Rule 27 was abolished.

Another rule, which led to much criticism of the association, was Rule 21. This forbade members of the British army or the RIC, the police force in Northern Ireland, to belong to the GAA and play its games. When peace was established in Northern Ireland this rule, too, was abolished in November 2001.

There was one other rule, which led to much criticism of the organisation. This was the rule which forbade the playing of 'foreign' games in Croke Park. Again the term 'foreign' seemed to apply exclusively to soccer and rugby. American Football had been played at the ground and a major boxing contest was held there. It was also used for concerts and other events.

When Lansdowne Road, the venue for soccer and rugby internationals featuring the Republic of Ireland teams, was marked down for redevelopment, the debate began about allowing soccer and rugby internationals to be played at Croke Park. Again after much heated debate the GAA decided to allow both codes to play there. In 2007 both soccer and rugby internationals took place in Croke Park.

Both occasions were of momentous importance. They showed how far the GAA had moved in the intervening years. Both were also occasions when the magnificent stadium that is Croke Park, one of the finest in Europe, could be seen and admired by people from all over the world.

The Future of the GAA

At the start of this new millennium the GAA is stronger than ever and is without doubt the most important sporting organisation in Ireland. There are around 2,000 clubs in the country. Most have first class facilities and have the support of the local population. Games are attracting huge numbers of spectators and there is widespread television coverage of major tournaments. Ladies' football is gaining popularity year by year and camogie still commands strong support.

Handball, which is the least known and played of all the games the association supports, is gaining in popularity. In many areas, old ball alleys have been redeveloped. It is played internationally and Ireland has had great success in recent years. This bodes well for the game and it is not beyond possibility that with proper promotion and television coverage, it could become a very important sport indeed.

The GAA faces many difficulties in the coming years. There is always the threat from other games. There are many more ways now for people to spend their leisure time. Young people have greater opportunities to take part in other sports. Television and video games keep young people inside more and more and cause them to lead much less active lives. Many now play far less sport than did the younger people of past generations.

The GAA has also to face the problem of professionalism in the game. There is now much more money involved than there was in the past. Sponsorship and television has increased greatly the GAA's revenues. The players, who after all provide the entertainment for the huge crowds and television audiences, do not get paid. Many are now demanding that they should be paid and have set up their own organisations to look after their welfare. It seems inevitable that at some time in the future there will be confrontation between the association and the players over this matter.

But yet the GAA is in a much better position than it has ever been in the past. Every year, tens of thousands of people, young and old, take part in GAA games and other activities promoted by the association. Spectators at the games are counted in the millions. Millions more watch the games worldwide on television and lately on the Internet. Still others listen to radio commentaries.

The All-Ireland Football and Hurling championships are still the biggest sporting events in the country. The standard of play has improved. The introduction of the back-door system, where defeated teams get a second chance, has brought a new dimension to the championship. In the matter of change, the GAA has always shown itself to be ready to embrace any development that will enhance the games it supports.

But the great secret of its success has been the support it receives in parishes, villages, towns and cities all over Ireland. In almost all communities it is still one of the most important aspects of life. It can still arouse passion in communities and the fervour that a match between children from rival parishes generates can be on a par with the sort of passion encountered between rival supporters in Croke Park on any All-Ireland final Sunday.

While that passion and rivalry continues, and while ordinary people from all walks of life support their parish and their county – win, lose or draw – the GAA, which Michael Cusack founded on that November Saturday in 1884, will continue to thrive. It has undoubtedly been one of the most influential and important organisations in Ireland in the last hundred years and no doubt will continue to do so into this new millennium.

THE HISTORY OF HURLING

The Legends

The game of hurling is as old as the myths and legends of Ireland. It has been played for thousands of years, though it is very unlikely that the ancient game bears much resemblance to the game of hurling we see today.

One of the earliest legends associated with hurling is that of the ancient Irish hero, Setanta. He lived in Ulster and as a child was never without his hurley or ball with which he continually practised his skills. Even when travelling he took a hurley and a ball with him. As he walked along he would puck the sliotar ahead of him, then throw his spear after the ball and run to catch both before they fell to the ground.

As a boy, he attended a school at the court of King Conchur of Ulster. Here the game of hurling was encouraged and Setanta became the school's star player. When King Conchur was invited to a banquet at the home of Culann, a blacksmith, he decided to take Setanta with him. Setanta was playing a game of hurling at the time and told the king that he would follow him when the game was over. Later, when the game had finished, Setanta set off for the house of Culann.

Meanwhile, the king had arrived at the house of Culann. Once there, his host had asked the king if all his guests had arrived. The king, forgetting about Setanta, assured Culann that they had arrived. Culann then ordered that his most fearsome hound, which acted as a guard dog, be released.

Setanta eventually arrived at Culann's house where he was faced by this fearsome hound. But being brave and quick thinking, he took immediate action that saved his life. With extraordinary speed and accuracy, he struck the ball with his hurley into the baying hound's mouth and deep down its throat. The ball stuck in the hound's throat and it choked to death.

On hearing the baying of the hound, King Conchur remembered Setanta. He, like Culann and the other guests in the house, thought that Setanta would be savaged to death by the beast. They rushed outside, dreading the worst, only to find the hound dead and Setanta unharmed.

Naturally, Culann was angry at the death of his guard dog. Setanta, too, was horrified at having killed the hound. To make up for it, he offered to become Culann's guard dog or hound until a new hound could be found and trained. Setanta also changed his name to that of 'Cú Chulainn', which means the hound of Culann.

Another legend tells of Labhraidh Loinseach, King of Leinster, who was born dumb. His father had consulted many experts in medicine and various healers, but none could help the boy to speak. But one day, while playing a game of hurling, Labhraidh was struck on the shin by a hurley. The pain was so intense that the boy cried out and afterwards was able to speak.

While these stories and many more like them are part of legend, there are many actual official references to hurling being played in olden times. The Brehon Laws, which date back to around the year 800 AD, had laws relating to hurling. The Statutes of Kilkenny, around 1366–67, forbade the playing of the game of hurling. Luckily those laws, or like the sixteenth-century Statutes of Galway (which forbade the playing of hurling), did not succeed, and the game continued to be played down through the centuries.

The Revival of Hurling

Around the eighteenth century there were two forms of hurling being played in Ireland. The first was played mostly in Leinster and Munster. It was called 'camán', or 'iománaíocht', a game similar to the game we know today. In this game, the ball could be struck along the ground by the hurley, but it could also be picked up, held in the hand and struck from there.

The second form, which was mostly played in the north of Ireland, was called 'camánacht'. The hurley used in this game resembled the hockey stick we see today. The ball could be struck along the ground with the stick but could not be picked up and held in the hand. Today in Scotland they still play this type of game, which is called 'shinty'.

Hurling survived all the various attempts to ban it and was popular until the nineteenth century. There are numerous reports of games, and songs and ballads exist which praise the exploits of teams and recount famous matches. Most of these matches were organised by landlords where one estate would play another. Betting was popular and large sums of money would be wagered on the outcome.

The History of Hurling

But by the beginning of the nineteenth century, hurling went into decline. The rebellion of 1798 was one reason for this. Another reason was poverty and the terrible Famine of 1845–48.

By 1884, when Michael Cusack and his supporters met to set up the GAA, the game of hurling was in real danger of extinction. It was still being played in Munster and in east Galway, and in County Antrim in the north of Ireland. It was also being played in Dublin and one of the main teams there was Cusack's Dublin Metropolitan Hurling Club.

On Easter Monday, 13 April 1884, Cusack brought his club to Ballinasloe, County Galway, to play a local team, Killimor. The match was played on the Fair Green in the town and was watched by a large crowd. At this time there were no defined rules and the match ended in a dispute over a score. This made Cusack realise that if native Irish games were to survive then strict rules would have to be drawn up and enforced throughout the country.

Rules for the playing of hurling games were drawn up by the newly formed GAA in January 1885. These, of course, have changed with the passage of years and the rules we see today will no doubt change in the future as the game evolves. One of the most important rules drawn up for both football and hurling was the rule of one team to one parish and that a player must come from a parish in order to be eligible to play for that team.

After the founding of the GAA, parishes began to form teams. Nearby parishes then formed their own teams. Inter-club matches became popular and gradually games between teams from different counties began to be organised. Such was the success of the venture that an inter-county championship began in 1887. This was between club teams and five counties took part: Galway,

Clare, Tipperary, Wexford and Kilkenny. In the final Tipperary beat Galway to become the first All-Ireland hurling champions.

It was a beginning. In those days, the players usually played in long trousers and vests and many often wore caps. In one game, a team from Cork played in their bare feet! It makes one wonder what their toes looked like at the final whistle.

Cork was the first county to win three All-Irelands in a row in the years 1892–94. This achievement was matched by Tipperary in 1898–1900. It was start of a great tradition in the All-Ireland championship for both counties and they were to go on to be two of the great hurling counties of all time.

At this time, games were played at different venues throughout the country. But, in 1895, the final between Tipperary and Kilkenny was of great significance. It was the first final to be played at Jones' Road, later to become the most famous of all GAA grounds, known today worldwide as Croke Park.

Another famous and historic hurling final took place at Jones' Road in August 1903 between Redmonds, representing Cork, and a team representing London. This game was actually the final of the 1901 hurling championship. In 1900 teams from England were allowed to take part in the All-Ireland championship. This was the first time a team from outside Ireland won an All-Ireland Senior Hurling final with London defeating Cork 1-5 to 0-4. Since then no team from outside the country has won an All-Ireland Senior Hurling Championship.

At the beginning of the twentieth century another county came to the fore in hurling. This was Kilkenny and they were to go on to be one of the major hurling counties. Indeed as the game progressed, a certain number of teams began to dominate the game. In Connacht, it was Galway that came to the fore. In Ulster, Antrim and Down were the main teams. Leinster had Dublin, Kilkenny and Wexford. In Munster there were five noted teams: Clare, Limerick, Cork, Tipperary and Waterford. These teams between them have dominated hurling and have won the majority of titles.

At first there were twenty-one players on a team, then seventeen, but when Kilkenny won the All-Ireland in 1913 the number had been reduced to fifteen, a figure that still applies today. Playing on that Kilkenny team were the Doyle brothers, who won eighteen All-Ireland medals between them. It's a record that still stands. Indeed, sets of brothers have featured in many great teams down through the years.

In 1912, the GAA set up an All-Ireland Junior championship. Cork were the first winners, defeating Westmeath in the final 3-6 to 2-1. Sixteen years later, in 1928, a Minor championship was also set up. Here again in the first final Cork were the winners, beating Dublin in a replay 7-6 to 4-0.

The Liam McCarthy Cup

In the 1921 All-Ireland final, Limerick made hurling history when they easily defeated Dublin 8-5 to 3-2. The match was not played until March 1923 because of the Civil War. The historic moment came when the Liam McCarthy Cup was presented to the Limerick captain, Bob McConkey. It was the first time the cup was presented to a winning captain. Now it is the most famous trophy in hurling and the one all hurlers want to win.

Another landmark in the game of hurling came in 1925–26 with the setting up of the National League. Cork once more won the first final where they beat Dublin 3-7 to 1-5. The win was to signal the beginning of a great era for Cork hurling.

In the twenty years between 1906 and 1926, no team had dominated the championship. But now a great Cork team arrived on the scene. In the next six years they won four All-Ireland titles and two National League titles. In the 1928 final they beat Galway in a record score of 6-12 to 1-0. This record-winning margin of 27 points was equalled in 1943, again by Cork. In that final they beat Antrim 5-16 to 0-4. This record-winning margin of 27 points still stands and it is unlikely that it will ever be beaten.

In 1927 the GAA set up another hurling tournament. This was the Railway Cup competition, which was played between provincial teams chosen from the best players in the four provinces. Leinster won the first competition on St Patrick's Day 1927 when they defeated Munster 1-11 to 2-6. Those who watched that game afterwards claimed it was the greatest game of hurling they had ever seen. The Munster team, well represented by players from the great Cork team, had their revenge in the following four years in a row, when they defeated Leinster in the final.

In fact, both provinces dominated the competition and it was not until 1944 that another province, Connacht, dominated by players from Galway, appeared in a final. In the following year, Ulster appeared for the first time. In 1947 Connacht was the first team outside the 'big two' to win the Railway Cup. This is a good indicator that Leinster and Munster were the two strong hurling areas in the country. In this modern era both provinces still dominate hurling.

The 1930s saw the emergence of two great hurling teams. Kilkenny played in a total of eight All-Ireland finals in that decade and won four. But the team best remembered from that era is Limerick. They played in a total of five finals and won three. They also set another record in that time, which has never been equalled. This was in the National League where they won five titles in a row. In those years they won a total of 35 league games in a row, a terrific achievement.

The Limerick and Kilkenny teams from that time are remembered for another reason – both had a star player. On the Kilkenny team was the great Lory Meagher while Limerick had Mick Mackey. There are still some hurling fans and players who rate Mackey as the best hurler of all time.

The Era of Cork and Christy Ring

The next era in hurling belonged to Cork and Christy Ring, undoubtedly the greatest hurler of all time. The first of Cork's appearances in the final was in 1941. They won that final and went on to win the following three finals, making them the first team to win four All-Irelands in a row. Since then no team has won four in a row and it seems certain that Cork's record will stand for a long time yet. In the years 1941–47 Cork appeared in six finals and won five.

The end of the 1940s saw Tipperary win three All-Irelands in a row. Then Cork came back to win another three in a row. This great Cork team, which won five titles in the 1940s and the three-in-a-row in the 1950s have, like Kilkenny and Limerick before them, another claim to fame.

Christy Ring, almost universally regarded as the greatest hurler of all time, played on that Cork team. He won eight All-Ireland

The legendary Christy Ring. ('Irish Independent')

medals and captained the team in three finals. Also on that Cork team was another hurler who won eight All-Ireland medals. This was Jack Lynch, regarded as one of the finest midfielders of all time.

Jack Lynch went on to greater fame when he was later elected Taoiseach, the head of the Irish government.

In the 1950s, a new challenger for All-Ireland honours emerged. This was Wexford. They had won their first All-Ireland title in 1910, defeating Limerick by 7-0 to 6-2. They appeared again in the final in 1918, but Limerick had their revenge and won easily. After that, Wexford did not appear in a final until 1951, when they lost to Tipperary, who were winning their third final in a row. Wexford's next appearance was in the 1954 final when a Cork team with Christy Ring as captain, and going for three in a row, beat them.

In fact, Wexford only won two All-Ireland titles in the 1950s, in 1955 and 1956, a record that hardly merits a claim to fame. But such was the excitement generated by this team that they drew record attendances at matches. In the 1954 final a record crowd of nearly 85,000 watched the match. Wexford also set records for National League attendances when over 45,000 watched the 1955 final.

Wexford's win in 1956 is memorable for a number of reasons. In that final, Christy Ring was going for a record ninth All-Ireland medal. Towards the end of the game he burst through on goal with only the Wexford goalkeeper, Art Foley, to beat. Foley brilliantly saved a certain goal and struck a long ball downfield. It was picked up by Nicky Rackard, who burst through the Cork defence to score a terrific match-winning goal for Wexford.

Christy Ring was so impressed with Art Foley's save that he congratulated the goalkeeper. But when the game was over Ring was accorded an unusual honour. He was grabbed by two Wexford players, Bobbie Rackard and Nick O'Donnell, and carried shoulder-high from the field. It was a fitting honour for the greatest hurler of them all.

In that era Wexford also won two National League titles and supplied the bulk of the players for Leinster in the Railway Cup final winning teams of 1954 and 1956. Wexford were an exciting, attacking team that played with great flair and skill. They entertained the huge crowds that came to watch them play and are rightly remembered as one of the most exciting hurling teams of all time.

Tipperary to the Fore

The late 1950s and on into the 1960s was the great era of Tipperary. They played in eight All-Ireland finals and won five. They were also the most successful team in the National League and won three titles in a row in this period. At the heart of the team were John and Jimmy Doyle, the former a winner of eight All-Ireland medals. Even today they are still regarded as one of the best hurling teams of all time.

Only one new team made a breakthrough in this period of almost total Tipperary dominance and this was Waterford. They had won their first All-Ireland title in 1948 when they beat Dublin. Then in the final of 1959, they beat Kilkenny in a replay 3-12 to 1-10. On this Waterford team was the great Tom Cheasty, still regarded as one of the games' best players.

The 1970 All-Ireland between Cork and Wexford set a record for the highest number of scores in any final, Cork winning 6-21 to 5-10. The 1971 final holds the record for the second highest number of scores with Tipperary beating Kilkenny 5-17 to 5-14. This match has one other claim to fame, as it was the first final to be shown in colour on television.

In the 1970s only one new team broke the hold of the 'big three' of Cork, Tipperary and Kilkenny. This occurred in 1973 when Limerick won the All-Ireland title beating Kilkenny 1-21 to 1-14. But hope of a Limerick revival to match that of the 1930s was dashed the following year when Kilkenny had their revenge.

The Kilkenny team who played Limerick in the All-Ireland Senior Hurling final in 1973. Front row (l–r): P. Broderick, P. Lawlor, M. Brennan, L. O'Brien, P. Delaney, N. Skehan, C. Dunne, F. Larkin; back row (l–r): N. Orr, P. Cullen, B. Cody, P. Henderson, M. Crotty, F. Cummins, J. Lynch. ('Irish Examiner')

Breakthrough of Galway, Offaly and Clare

The 1980 All-Ireland final is notable for two reasons. It was the first time since 1955 that one of the 'big three' teams didn't make it to the final, which was played between Galway and Limerick.

The second significant point about this final was that it marked the breakthrough of Galway.

In fact, the 1980s marked a breakthrough for another team not noted for hurling success. This team was Offaly. They won their first All-Ireland title in 1981, beating the previous year's winners, Galway, 2-12 to 0-15. They were the first new winners of the Liam McCarthy Cup since Waterford's win in 1948. In 1985 they repeated this win in the final, again over Galway, 2-11 to 1-12, proving that though they were a new county on the hurling scene, they were here to stay.

The 1980s brought a huge change to the hurling championship. In this decade only two finals were contested between teams from the 'big three'. This occurred in 1982 and 1983 when Kilkenny beat Cork on both occasions. Tipperary made only two appearances in a final during the decade. 1989 saw another new county team, Antrim, appear in a final in Croke Park. However, it was to be a disappointing appearance for the team from Northern Ireland when they lost badly to Tipperary, 4-24 to 3-9.

The dominance of the 'big three' was again challenged in the 1990s by another team that brought huge excitement to the game of hurling. This was Clare. A legend surrounded the county that a woman named Biddy Early had cursed the county and that because of this they were destined never to win an All-Ireland title.

At the beginning of the 1990s hurling in Clare was at such a low ebb that many believed in the curse. Then a man called Ger Loughnane became their manager and was also destined to become one of the most controversial and colourful and, indeed, successful men in the game.

The History of Hurling

To the surprise of everyone, except Loughnane and the players, Clare won the Munster championship in 1995, the first in sixty-three years. In the All-Ireland semi-final they defeated Galway and set up a final meeting with Offaly. Trailing by two points with only minutes left, they again seemed destined to be victims of the curse. But a goal by Eamonn Taafe destroyed the legend of Biddy Early and, when the final whistle blew, Clare were All-Ireland champions. It had been eighty-one years since their last All-Ireland win and it seemed as if every hurling supporter in Ireland, with probably the exception of Offaly supporters, was overjoyed.

The success in the championship of teams other than the 'big three' of Cork, Tipperary and Kilkenny continued the following year, 1996, when Wexford beat Limerick in the final. In 1997 Clare were back again, this time beating Tipperary. 1997 was also the year when the back-door system was introduced and brought a new level of excitement to the game of hurling.

Under this new system, the losing Munster and Leinster finalists were allowed back into the competition. As there are only a handful of counties capable of winning an All-Ireland Senior hurling title, there is fierce rivalry among the main contenders. Now this rivalry increased when beaten teams were given a second chance. In 1997 Clare and Tipperary, fierce Munster rivals, both made it to the final, thus intensifying the excitement and anticipation of all hurling fans. There have been changes made to the back-door system since 1997, but the excitement generated by it has not diminished.

1998 is remembered for all the wrong reasons. In the All-Ireland semi-final, Clare played Offaly. Unfortunately, the referee blew the final whistle before the time was up, giving Clare victory. Offaly supporters invaded the pitch and staged a sit-down. The

GAA ordered that the game be replayed and in the replay Offaly won and went on to defeat Kilkenny in the final.

The Future of Hurling in the New Millennium

If the last two decades of the twentieth century had seen the emergence of new teams, the beginning of the new millennium has seen the emergence of the old powers once more. Cork and Kilkenny have dominated the decade and each has prevented the other from winning three All-Ireland championships in a row. The only team to make a breakthrough in this decade have been Waterford. They have excited crowds all over the country with their stylish play and have added names like Brown, McGrath, Mullane, Shanahan and Kelly to the list of greats. But though they have won a National League title, the longed for All-Ireland crown has so far eluded them.

In the 2008 All-Ireland final Waterford played a Kilkenny team going for a three-in-a-row, and were heavily defeated in what many have described as the finest display of hurling ever seen in Croke Park. Kilkenny achieved their three-in-a-row and are now being compared to the great Cork, Limerick and Tipperary teams of the past, with their star player, Henry Shefflin, being compared to the great Christy Ring. At the moment, Kilkenny seem unbeatable for the foreseeable future and that worries many of those who love the game of hurling.

But there is much to be optimistic about too. The emergence of new champions and challengers and the introduction of the back-door system have brought a new excitement to the game. To their credit, the GAA have tried to revitalise hurling in those other counties that do not normally feature in the All-Ireland championships. They have introduced the Nicky Rackard Cup and the

The History of Hurling

Christy Ring Cup as alternative championships for the weaker counties. And though no new county has yet emerged from these competitions to challenge the powerful hurling counties, perhaps this will occur in the not too distant future.

Yet hurling is still the fastest and most exciting field game in the world. The level of skill shown by the players is breathtaking and in recent times we've had the pleasure of watching some of the greatest hurling matches of all time. While players show such high levels of skill and bring such excitement to the huge crowds that come to watch the matches, the game of hurling will survive. Indeed with the advent of satellite television the ancient game of hurling may yet one day take its place on a world stage, and become to be regarded, as it is by Irish people everywhere, as the greatest field game in the whole world.

HURLING GREATS

Christy Ring

Setanta belongs to the ancient legends and folklore of Ireland. Christy Ring, on the other hand, belongs to modern folklore and legend. If any hurler can rightly be described as 'the greatest there has ever been', that man is Christy Ring, or Ringey, the nickname by which he was sometimes known.

He was one of those players who would draw a crowd that came just to see him play. Even opposition supporters would be disappointed if he wasn't on the rival team, though his presence was almost a guarantee that their team would be beaten.

Ring was born in Cloyne, County Cork, in October 1920. From when he was big enough to hold a hurley, he was hardly ever without it. He endlessly practised the skills of the game until one might believe he had been born with a hurley in his hands.

Born at a time of great poverty and political turmoil in Ireland, he left school at fourteen. He trained as a motor mechanic and later worked as an oil tanker driver. He always carried a hurley in his cab and at lunchtime would stop along the road, hop into the nearest field and practise his hurling skills. It was his skill and brilliance, sharpened by countless hours of practice and then displayed on the hurling pitch that earned him his fame.

His achievements have never been surpassed. He won eight All-Ireland Senior Hurling medals and nine Munster Championship medals. He played for Glen Rovers when he moved to Cork city and won fourteen Cork Championships with them. He holds the record for Railway Cup wins, eighteen in all, a record that surely will never be surpassed.

Ring was not a tall man but he was immensely strong. Yet for such a powerfully built man he was fast and nimble on his feet. He could pick up the ball on the run, sidestep an opponent and smash the ball into the net in the blink of an eye. On one occasion he scored three goals in almost as many minutes.

Even today, when so many more great goals have been scored, he is still credited with the finest All-Ireland goal of all time. He scored this goal against Cork's great rivals, Kilkenny, in Croke Park in 1946. Getting the ball near the halfway line, Ring raced through the Kilkenny defence. With the ball hopping on the end of his hurley, he flashed past the defenders before beating the goalkeeper with a well-timed flick.

Christy Ring died in 1979. Songs, poems and books have been written of his exploits. Films telling his life story have been made. Statues have been erected to his memory and a bridge in Cork city is named after him.

When the greatest hurling team of the first hundred years of the GAA was chosen in 1984, Christy Ring was an automatic choice. He was also an automatic choice on the Team of the Millennium in 2000 and he has been elected to the GAA's Hall of Fame.

But it is for his skills on the hurling field that he is most remembered today and he rightly claims his place as the greatest hurler of all time. It is often said of a great person that his likes will never been seen again. That accolade might have been written especially for Christy Ring.

Mick Mackey

Limerick has produced some great hurlers but none as great as Mick Mackey. He was the ultimate showman and had the skills and bravery and talent to go with it. Like Ringey, his presence alone on the Limerick team would draw huge crowds to games.

He was born in 1912 in Castleconnell, just outside Limerick city, and worked for the Electricity Supply Board as a van driver. The Mackey family was very much involved in the GAA. Both Mick's grandfather and father, the latter who was known by the nickname 'Tyler', were well-known Limerick hurlers. Mick's brother, John, was also a noted hurler and both brothers won numerous honours while playing together for Limerick and for their club, Ahane.

At the time the Mackey brothers were playing, Ahane was one of the most successful hurling and football clubs in the county. This was due in no small part to the presence of the two brothers. With Ahane, Mick Mackey won fifteen County Championship medals. He was also a noted footballer and won five County Championship football medals as well.

Mackey was the star of the Limerick hurling team of the 1930s. That team is still regarded today as the finest hurling team of that decade. It was certainly a golden age for hurling in County Limerick.

Hurling Greats

Between 1930 and 1940, Limerick won five Munster Championships. They also won three All-Ireland titles, beginning with the county's fourth title in 1934. In 1936 they won again with Mick Mackey as captain. In 1940 he again captained Limerick to All-Ireland victory over Kilkenny. The team also won five National League titles in a row between 1934 and 1938, a terrific achievement.

Mick Mackey had great skills as a hurler. He was powerful and quick and rarely missed pulling on a ball whether it was on the ground or in the air. But it was for his solo runs that he was rightly famous. These thrilled crowds, Limerick fans and opposition fans alike. When he ran at defenders with the ball seemingly attached to the end of his hurley, he brought crowds to their feet.

Mick Mackey died in 1982 and his funeral was one of the biggest seen in County Limerick. Former players, both his fellow Limerick hurlers and opponents, came to pay their respects to one of the greats. Such was Mick Mackey's prowess on the hurling field that, like Ringey, he was also included in the Team of the Century and the Team of the Millennium.

The Rackard Brothers

Brothers feature strongly in the annals of hurling, as indeed do sisters in camogie. One of the most famous sets of brothers of all time are the three Rackards from Wexford. Bobby, Billy and Nicky, the most famous of them all. Nicky played at full-forward and was the scourge of full-backs during Wexford's great hurling era, the 1950s.

Kilkenny was the dominant hurling team in Leinster at that time. Wexford had not appeared in an All-Ireland in over thirty years. They had lost to Limerick in 1918 when counties were still represented by club teams. But in the era of the 1950s, inspired by the Rackard brothers, Wexford rose to greatness.

It began in 1951 when they reached their first All-Ireland final since that 1918 defeat. Their opponents were Tipperary and though Wexford played well, they ended up on the losing side. They were well beaten in Leinster in the following two years and it seemed as if they were forever destined to be losers. In 1954 they again reached the final and again were beaten, this time by Cork.

But in 1955 they eventually won an All-Ireland title, beating Galway in the final. Such was the standard of their hurling and the excitement they generated that they drew the largest crowds to any All-Ireland final, thrilling them with their great skills. They won again in 1956, beating the great Cork team of that era with a match-winning goal from Nicky Rackard.

The Rackard brothers were from Rathnure. Nicky was regarded as the finest full-forward of all time. His speciality was scoring goals from frees with unstoppable shots. In 1956 Wexford and the Rackard brothers probably had their greatest victory when they beat Tipperary in the National League final. They were behind by fifteen points at one stage but rallied to win by eight points.

Nicky was a scoring machine and his totals in games, both of goals and points, seem unbelievable today. In one game against Antrim he scored an amazing seven goals and seven points. No modern player has ever matched his totals and it is unlikely that they ever will. Nicky, who died in 1975, when he was only fifty-three years of age, was further honoured by being chosen at full-forward on the Team of the Century.

Hurling Greats

Both Bobby and Billy Rackard also featured on that great Wexford team that won two All-Ireland titles in 1955 and 1956. Billy also won a third Senior All-Ireland medal in 1960. They also won National League and Railway Cup medals. Bobby, too, was honoured by being picked on the Team of the Millennium. The achievement of the three brothers, Bobby, Billy and Nicky, rightly grants them the accolade of being regarded as one of the finest sets of brothers ever to play hurling.

The Doyles of Tipperary

County Tipperary has produced some great hurlers. Two of its finest players were John and Jimmy Doyle. Though they shared the same surname, they were not related and achieved their fame from very different positions on the field.

John Doyle was an only son and was born in Holycross in 1930. His mother died soon after his birth and he was reared by his father, who was a farmer. John soon showed an interest in hurling where he played at corner-back, not an ideal position from which to win glory. Yet he was such a terrifically talented hurler that he earned the right to be considered with the greats like Ring and Mackey.

John began his claim to fame in September 1949 when, at nineteen years of age, he played in his first All-Ireland final in Croke Park. Laois were Tipperary's opponents that day and Tipperary won easily. It was to be the first of a three-in-a-row winning sequence of All-Irelands for that Tipperary team.

John Doyle received the first of his eight medals that day, a total that equals the tally of the great Christy Ring. John also won eleven National League medals and ten Munster Senior hurling medals and regularly played for Munster in the Railway Cup, winning even more medals and glory.

He was a very strong, powerful defender, known to be a hard tackler and well able to burst out of defence and put Tipperary on the attack. He was feared by all corner-forwards and there were many who heaved a sigh of relief when John retired after the 1967 All-Ireland final in which an ageing Tipperary team were beaten by their great rivals, Kilkenny.

Such was John Doyle's reputation that he was chosen as the Texaco Hurler of the Year, an award that more often than not goes to a midfielder or forward. He was an automatic choice when the

Team of the Century and the Team of the Millennium were chosen, an accolade worthy of one of the greatest defenders the game has ever known.

Jimmy Doyle was born in Thurles, County Tipperary, in 1940. Such was his early promise that he made his debut on the Tipperary minor team, aged only fourteen. He was one of the greatest hurling forwards of all time and can be ranked among the likes of Mackey and Ring.

The year 1965 was a remarkable one for both the Doyles and Tipperary. In the All-Ireland final that year Tipperary beat Wexford. It was the

Tipperary captain, Jimmy Doyle, picured here at Croke Park before the All-Ireland Senior Hurling final of 1969. (Sportsfile)

county's twenty-first All-Ireland win, a notable achievement, and saw John Doyle win his eighth Senior medal. Jimmy, as captain of the winning team, was presented with the McCarthy Cup. It was the fulfilment of a dream and made up for a previous disappointment.

In 1962 Tipperary won the All-Ireland final. Jimmy Doyle was captain. But before the end of the game he was injured. He broke his collarbone and had to be carried off. Unable to go up to receive the cup, Tony Wall received the cup instead. It was a great disappointment for Jimmy and so the 1965 final was even more special for him.

Jimmy won the first of his six All-Ireland Senior Hurling medals in 1958 when aged only eighteen. In that game he scored five points. He won again in 1960, though he played with an injured ankle, which almost kept him out of the game.

When Jimmy Doyle is remembered today it is for his scoring accuracy. He could score freely from play from any forward position on the field. But he is equally well remembered for his deadly accuracy from frees. It was a skill honed as a young boy when he spent hours practising at Semple Stadium, a stone's throw from where he was born.

When he retired in 1973, his speed and agility beginning to be destroyed by arthritis, Jimmy was the Tipperary goalkeeper. This was a position he had once played in as a young man. No doubt there is many a defender who wished that Jimmy Doyle had remained a goalkeeper instead of becoming one of the most feared attacking forwards of all time.

Like John Doyle, Jimmy Doyle was chosen on the Team of the Century and the Team of the Millennium. It was a fitting tribute to one of the greatest forwards in the game of hurling.

The Story of the GAA

Eddie Keher

Kilkenny is rightly regarded as probably the greatest of all the hurling counties. It has produced some great players down through the years, but few to match the skills and the free-taking abilities of Eddie Keher. Many would regard him as the finest and most accurate free taker in the history of the game.

He was born in Inistioge near Thomastown in 1941 and first came to prominence with the Rower/Inistioge Club. Even as a minor on the Kilkenny team, he stood out from all the others. Such was his talent that he played for both the Minor team and the Senior team in the 1959 All-Ireland finals. Waterford won the Senior final that year in a replay but Eddie Keher had his revenge four years later. Kilkenny beat Waterford in 1963 with Eddie Keher scoring 14 points, ten of them from frees.

It was the first of his many Senior achievements, which include six All-Ireland medals. He also won three National League medals, was Hurler of the Year in 1972 and won All-Star Awards five years in a row. He is one of the highest scorers of all time and his tallies of goals and points will hardly ever be surpassed. In numerous seasons he was the top scorer in hurling. He also held the record for the highest score in an All-Ireland Senior final until 1989 when Nicky English scored 2-12 in the final against Antrim, a record which is unlikely to be broken in the near future – if, indeed, it ever will be.

After twenty-one years of faithful service to Kilkenny hurling, Eddie Keher retired in 1977. While many a defender sighed with relief, hurling supporters of all colours heard the news with great regret. Never again would they see Eddie Keher flit through defences as if he were a ghost before crashing the ball into the net. No more would they see his deadly accuracy from frees, some from angles that would have proved impossible for other men. One of the truly greats had left the game but his name and the memories of his achievements would live on.

Eddie Keher in action against Cork in the All-Ireland Senior Hurling final at Croke Park, 7 September 1969.

D. J. Carey

D. J. Carey is regarded by many hurling enthusiasts as one of the greatest hurlers of all time, another man who deserves to be compared with Christy Ring and Mick Mackey. It is always difficult to make comparisons but it can certainly be said that D. J. is ranked among the greats of the modern era.

Nicknamed 'the Dodger' for obvious reasons, he spent his great hurling years dodging the unfortunate defenders who were given the job of marking him. When he was at the height of his hurling prowess, there was no defender capable of marking him.

D. J., like the great Jimmy Doyle, began his hurling career as a goalkeeper. He was an all-round sportsman and excelled at football and handball as well as hurling. Indeed he is also regarded as one of the finest handball players of all time.

Success came early to D. J. He won All-Ireland Colleges titles and Minor and U-21 All-Ireland medals before bursting onto the Senior Kilkenny team. He possessed great confidence, as befitting a star in the making, and was fast, agile and deadly accurate both from play and from frees. He was also a noted penalty taker. But it was seeing D. J. racing towards goal, his hurley held short in his hand, the ball seemingly glued to the bas, that thrilled the crowds that came to see him play.

D. J. won his first Senior All-Ireland medal in 1992 and added a second in 1993 when he was voted Hurler of the Year. Seven years would pass before Kilkenny won another All-Ireland Senior title. But in those barren years, one hurler stood head and shoulders above any other. That man was D. J. Carey.

D. J. had won All-Star Awards in 1991, 1992 and 1993, as befitting the star player in a successful team which had appeared in three finals in a row, winning two of them. But in the following years, when Kilkenny were no longer a power in hurling, D. J. won All-Star Awards in 1994, 1995, 1997 and again in 2000 when he also won his third All-Ireland Senior medal. On that day, Kilkenny, facing a third successive defeat in a final, thrashed Offaly. D. J. was named Man of the Match and again was voted Hurler of the Year.

Hurling Greats

The year 2000 was the Millennium Year and a hurling team of the greats of the game was chosen to mark the occasion. To the surprise and the dismay of many hurling fans, and especially those in Kilkenny, D. J. was not picked. It was probably one of the most controversial decisions made when the team was chosen. Perhaps his tally of only three All-Ireland Senior medals stood against him. But he played at a time when Kilkenny hurling was at an all-time low. Yet despite this, he was the finest player of that era.

In recent times the GAA has set up a Hall of Fame. Names like Ring and Mackey are already there. In years to come the name of D. J. Carey will surely be added and then he will take his rightful place among the hurling greats. They are the men who have graced the game with their skills and left spectators enthralled. They are the men who ensured and continue to ensure that the game of hurling continues to be the most exciting field game in the world.

D. J. Carey at the All-Ireland final in Croke Park in 2003. ('Irish Examiner')

HISTORY OF FOOTBALL

Early History and Rules

Gaelic football does not have the same ancient origins as hurling. Some of the earliest written references only date back to the Statutes of Galway, which were laws passed in that city in the sixteenth century. These laws forbade the playing of hurling, but for some unknown reason they did not forbid the playing of football. In later centuries, an increasing number of written references to the game can be found. There are also many songs and poems commemorating great games, which show that football was becoming an important part of Irish pastimes.

An early version of the game, in which a ball was used, was called Caid. It was very popular, particularly in Kerry. The ball usually consisted of the inflated bladder of an animal, most probably a pig, enclosed in sewn leather. Sometimes the sewn leather pouch was stuffed with hay or straw. In the game of Caid, a team would try to carry a ball from their parish or village area to a neighbouring village or parish. The neighbouring village or parish would attempt to stop the other team from doing so.

History of Football

Usually there was no limit to the number of players on either side. There were very few rules, indeed if any, and no referee. Wrestling and tripping were allowed and quite often the game ended with the players fighting each other.

Betting played a large part in most sporting events and it is likely that more organised football matches became popular for this reason. These matches would be played in a confined space – usually a large field. Here again, tripping and wrestling were allowed and there were no formal rules. Games often ended with the players from both teams fighting over disputed scores.

But due to rebellion and famine, the game of football declined and by 1880 it had almost died out in Ireland. At this time a new English game – rugby – was gaining popularity among soldiers, policemen and the middle class. It is likely that if Michael Cusack had not set up the GAA in 1884, the game of Gaelic football might have lost out to rugby and died out entirely.

But from the founding of the GAA, the game thrived and became even more popular than hurling. This was probably due to the fact that it was an easier game to master and only required a ball for play. In circumstances where a ball was not available one could be easily made. Hurling, on the other hand, demanded specific skills and one had also to possess a hurley, something not easily improvised, as well as a ball in order to play.

Though intended to organise athletics, by 1885 the GAA was already drawing up rules for the game of football. At first teams consisted of twenty-one players. This number was reduced to seventeen in 1892 and then to fifteen in 1913, the number that still applies today. Wrestling and tripping were banned, a referee and two umpires applied the rules and could order off any player who broke them.

The Story of the GAA

At first only goals were allowed. Later point-posts were introduced similar to those used today in Australian Rules Football. These two posts were set along the end line an equal distance from the goalposts. Any ball that went between those point-posts and the goalposts was deemed a point.

But points were only taken into consideration in determining the outcome of a game if no goals were scored or if each team scored an equal number of goals. So a team scoring one goal would beat a team with any number of points, but without a goal.

Eventually points began to count in deciding scores and at first a goal was deemed to be worth five points. Then, in 1896, the goal became the equivalent of three points and has remained so until the present time. In 1910 the point-posts were dispensed with and a point was scored when the ball went over the crossbar and between the two goalposts.

In the early years there were other differences to the rules we know today. There were no sideline kicks. Instead the ball was thrown in. There were no 'forty-fives' either. Instead a team forfeited, or lost, points. Then, in 1888, the fifty-yard free was introduced, then known as a 'fifty'. It has now become known as a 'forty-five' with the introduction of metric measures.

The GAA has always been open to rule changes to improve their Gaelic games and make them more exciting for the players and spectators alike. No doubt this will continue into the future and many of the rules we see today may disappear or change. This is necessary if the game is to remain strong and exciting. Football is a fast-paced, exciting game and rule changes that allow this to continue are to be welcomed.

History of Football

The All-Ireland Championship

The first All-Ireland Senior Football championship was held in 1887. Twelve teams entered but only eight actually took part and each county was represented by its top club team. The final, though, was not played until the following year, 1888. On 29 April, at Clonskeagh in Dublin, Limerick, represented by Limerick Commercials, defeated Dundalk Young Irelands, representing Louth, by 1-4 to 0-3. Limerick were then crowned as the first All-Ireland Gaelic Football champions.

There was no championship held in 1888. In that year both hurlers and footballers from Ireland travelled to the United States to play games there. It was the start of a tradition, which continues right up to the present.

The championship resumed in 1889 and Tipperary emerged as the winners. In fact in the early years of the All-Ireland Football championship, three teams not noted today for their football accomplishments regularly dominated. These were Limerick, Tipperary and Wexford. When we consider the great football teams of later times and of the present day, only Dublin and Cork had success in those early days. It was not until 1903, when Tralee Mitchels defeated London Hibernians in the final, that Kerry, the most successful county of all time, first won an All-Ireland title.

Dublin created history between 1887 and 1889 when they were the first team to win three All-Irelands in a row. Such was their dominance that they repeated this feat again between 1906 and 1908. But Wexford was to go one better than this between 1915 and 1918 when they were the first team to win four All-Irelands in a row. They were represented by a team known as the Blues and Whites with players drawn mostly from the New Ross area.

That success marked the end of Wexford's football dominance. Since then they have won only two Leinster titles, in 1945 and 2008, and have not won an All-Ireland final. Instead, it has been the Wexford hurlers who have brought success to the county.

By the 1920s Dublin and Kerry were beginning to dominate the All-Ireland championship with Dublin recording another three-in-a-row All-Ireland wins at the beginning of the decade. They were to create a rivalry with Kerry, which continues today and which has been responsible for some of the most memorable football games ever played.

Their 1923 final meeting, which gave Dublin their third three-in-a-row win, was the first one in which a club team did not represent either county. Now the best players from each county were picked and this brought a new dimension to the game. The 1923 final could be said to be the first genuine All-Ireland victory for a county team.

Few teams threatened the dominance of Kerry and Dublin during these years. Louth, Cork, Tipperary and Galway, the first Connacht county to win an All-Ireland in 1925 (though in controversial circumstances) did stop the 'big two'. One other great team from that era was Kildare.

The Sam Maguire Cup

The Kildare team of the 1920s is still regarded as one of the greatest teams of all time. They also have the distinction of being the first county to be presented with the Sam Maguire Cup, which is now the premier football trophy.

History of Football

Kildare won their first All-Ireland title in 1905 and added a second in 1919. But it was in the 1920s that they came to national prominence. In that decade they won six Leinster titles in a row and two All-Ireland titles, in 1927 and 1928. The 1928 final, between Kildare and Cavan, marked the historic moment when the Sam Maguire Cup was presented for the first time to Willie Gannon, the Kildare captain. That Kildare team has one other claim to fame: it was the first county to win two titles with the same team of players. Dublin is the only other team to achieve this, which they did in 1976 and 1977.

Kildare were going for a three-in-a-row in 1929 when they came up against a Kerry team regarded as one of the greatest football teams of all time. That 1929 win was the first of what was to be a four-in-a-row winning sequence for Kerry. In 1933 they were going for a historic five-in-a-row when they were beaten by Cavan in the semi-final. That year Cavan went on to create their own piece of GAA history by being the first team from Ulster to win an All-Ireland Football title when they defeated Galway 2-5 to 1-4.

New Competitions

In 1926 the National League was set up and the following year the Railway Cup competition began. Laois won the first National League title while Munster defeated Connacht on St Patrick's Day 1927 to win the first Railway Cup.

In the 1930s Mayo became the most successful National League winning team of all time. Between 1934 and 1939 they won a record six titles in a row and after Galway's win in 1940 came back to win again in 1941. That six-in-a-row winning sequence has not been matched and indeed is unlikely ever to be equalled. That great Mayo team also gave the county its first All-Ireland title in 1936.

In 1929, a Minor All-Ireland championship began. Clare emerged as surprising winners of that first final, defeating another surprising finalist, Longford, by 5-3 to 2-5. The Minor championship has also been dominated by the two top Gaelic football counties, Kerry and Dublin.

By 1939, Kerry were gaining dominance and had another three-in-a-row winning sequence between 1939–41. After that, no one team dominated the championship for the next twenty or so years. In these years a number of teams did win two All-Irelands in a row, including Kerry, Roscommon, Cavan, Mayo and Down.

One final played in this era has a special claim to fame. This was the 1947 final, the first and only one to be played outside the country. The final, between Kerry and Cavan, was played at the Polo Grounds in New York on Sunday 14 September 1947. A crowd of about 35,000 watched Cavan defeat Kerry by 2-11 to 2-7. Irish supporters at home had a chance to savour the occasion through listening to the commentary on the game by Micheál O'Hehir.

A Historic Breakthrough

In 1960 there was another historic moment in the annals of the GAA when Down won an All-Ireland title. In winning, they created history on a number of counts. It was the county's first All-Ireland title and the first time the Sam Maguire Cup went to a county from Northern Ireland. Their final appearances also created records for attendance at a final – over 90,000 were present in Croke Park in 1961 when they defeated Offaly to take their second title in a row. Down were to win yet another title in 1968 and are regarded by many of those who saw them as one of the most exciting Gaelic football teams of all time.

While the 1960s are rightly remembered for that great Down team and their breakthrough, they are also remembered for Galway's magnificent three-in-a-row All-Ireland wins between 1964 and 1966. That Galway team had Mattie McDonagh at centre-forward, the only Connacht player to win four All-Ireland medals, the first won on the Galway team that took the Sam Maguire Cup in 1956. In their historic three-in-a-row win they did not concede a single goal, thanks to Johnny Geraghty, one of the greatest goalkeepers of all time.

At the beginning of the 1970s, a new county made the breakthrough in football. This was Offaly, who won their first title in 1971 when they defeated Galway. They also won the following year, this time defeating Kerry and proving that they intended to be a force to be reckoned with. They are one of the few counties that have won both football and hurling All-Ireland titles, a terrific achievement for what is a relatively small county.

The All-Ireland Club championships were introduced in 1971. Kerry won the first title when the East Kerry club beat Bryansford. But the championships have been dominated by Cork teams Nemo Rangers and St Finbarrs. In 1971 an All-Stars Award system was set up with the intention of honouring the best players of each year. Although it sometimes generated controversy, it was a welcome addition to the GAA honours system as it recognised great players from counties that would rarely feature in major competitions.

The Story of the GAA

Dublin–Kerry Rivalry

While Offaly's breakthrough in the 1970s was a historic moment, the decade is remembered for the revival of football in Dublin and for their great rivalry with Kerry. It is probable that in that decade two of the finest football teams of all time came to the fore. Their rivalry created a passion and excitement that still lasts in the memory of those who saw them. Between 1974 and 1981 no other team won an All-Ireland title. Of the eight titles won, Kerry took five and Dublin three, and they played each other in four of those finals. Kerry won three of those games to Dublin's single victory.

The question is still asked today if that was the greatest Kerry team of all time. It is a question that can never really be answered. But that Kerry team deserves the accolade of being one of the greatest teams ever to play Gaelic football.

Between 1978 and 1981 they won four All-Ireland titles in a row, the second time they achieved this honour. In fact Kerry is the only county to achieve two four-in-a-row wins.

While that team is remembered for its achievements and for many great and memorable moments, one single moment stands out from all the rest. It came on 19 September 1982 in the dying moments of that year's All-Ireland final between Kerry and Offaly.

The previous year Kerry had beaten Offaly in the final, 1-12 to 0-8, to notch up that second four-in-a-row win. Now on this Sunday 19 September 1982, they were going for a record five titles in a row. Nearing the final whistle, Kerry seemed to be about to create history as they led Offaly by two points. Then a high ball dropped in towards the Kerry goalmouth. As Kerry fullback

History of Football

Tommy Doyle jumped for the ball he seemed to be nudged off it by Offaly forward Seamus Darby.

The referee did not blow his whistle for a foul and Seamus Darby smashed the ball into the Kerry net. The dream of a record five-in-a-row wins ended moments later when the referee blew the full-time whistle. Offaly had the sweetest of revenges for the previous year's defeat and showed other counties that they were a football force to be reckoned with. That Offaly team has one other claim to fame in that it had five sets of brothers in the squad.

In 1983 Kerry did not make it to the All-Ireland final and there were many who thought that the team had reached its pinnacle with its four-in-a-row win. But Kerry refused to accept defeat easily, and they were back in Croke Park in 1983 to beat Galway in the All-Ireland final. In the following two years they were back again, this time renewing their great rivalry with Dublin and beating them on both occasions to notch up yet another three-in-a-row win.

It was an extraordinary period for Kerry football. They played in eight out of nine All-Ireland finals between 1978 and 1986 and won seven of them. They were only denied a five-in-a-row by a brilliant though controversial goal. But for a team to win four-in-a-row and three-in-a-row All-Ireland titles in nine years is a remarkable achievement. Perhaps that record does confirm them as the greatest Gaelic football team of all time. Certainly it is a record that surely never will be equalled, never mind broken.

A New Exciting Era

The latter years of the 1980s and the early years of the 1990s saw the emergence of a fine team from Meath. It signalled the beginning of a great rivalry with Cork, who for years had been living in the shadow of Kerry. Meath and Cork had contested the 1967 All-Ireland final when Meath had emerged victorious. Now twenty years later in 1987 they played each other again. Meath again emerged as the winners, a feat they repeated in 1988.

Mayo had their first final win since 1951 in 1989, a gap of nearly forty years. Their opponents were Cork, now playing in their third final in a row. Cork emerged winners and in 1990 renewed their rivalry once more with Meath who had beaten the Munster team in 1987 and again in 1988. This time Cork had their revenge and won their second title in a row.

The following year, 1991, Meath were back in the final. On that day they were defeated by Down, which was the start of a new and exciting era, for football in Ulster. No Ulster team had won an All-Ireland since Down's win in 1968, and only one other Ulster team, Cavan, had won an All-Ireland title. All that was about to change as Ulster teams won the next four All-Irelands in a row. After Down's win in 1991 came a historic first for Donegal in 1992, then a first for Derry in 1993 before Down won again in 1994. In 1995, Tyrone contested the final but lost by a single point to Dublin. But Tyrone's day would come and confirm that Ulster was a force to be reckoned with.

Through the 1990s no team dominated the championship and there were eight different winners of the Sam Maguire Cup in the ten years. Only Down and Meath won two finals each while the big two of Kerry and Dublin had to be satisfied with one win each. Galway's win in 1998 was the first by a Connacht team since Galway's victory in 1966, thirty-two years earlier.

History of Football

The same pattern has continued since then with no one county dominating the championship, though Kerry have notched up more wins than any other team. There have also been new names added to the list of All-Ireland winners, namely Tyrone and Armagh. This has confirmed that Ulster is now a province to be reckoned with. In 2003 Ulster teams contributed a piece of history to the football championship when, for the first time, two teams from the same province contested the final, Tyrone beating Armagh 0-12 to 0-9.

This situation arose because of the introduction of the back-door system to the All-Ireland championship in 2001. Until then, the championship was played on a knockout basis. Once a team was beaten in their province, they were out of the championship for that year. This meant that many of the lesser counties only ever got the chance to play a single championship game each year. This did not bode well for those lesser counties. Not having the opportunity to play against the better teams, and to play regularly, they were destined not to have the chance to improve.

With the back-door system, teams beaten in the first round of their provincial championships were not automatically eliminated. These losing counties were drawn against each other in an open draw, thus having another opportunity to get further on in the championship. This led to four teams coming through this system. They would then play the four provincial champions in what became knows as the quarter-finals.

In 2001, Galway became the first football county to take advantage of this system. Though they were beaten by Roscommon in Connacht, they still came through the back-door qualifying rounds to reach the All-Ireland final where they beat

Meath. This system also led to the historic moment when Armagh and Tyrone, two counties from the same province contested the All-Ireland final.

The success of the system can be measured in the emergence of counties that have not featured prominently in the championship before and some that had not featured for a long time. Teams from Sligo, Fermanagh, Monaghan, Westmeath, Laois, Wexford and Limerick have benefited, and have also had the opportunity to play in Croke Park, the dream of every Gaelic footballer.

The fact that no one team has dominated the championship since Kerry's dominance back in the 1970s and 1980s has to be good for the future of Gaelic football. The emergence of the counties from Ulster, and Galway and Mayo's appearances in finals from Connacht, is also a good sign for the future. The back-door system has brought new hope for the lesser counties and has led to spectators from those counties and GAA supporters in general watching some of the most exciting football matches of recent times.

So at the beginning of the new millennium, and despite many difficulties facing Gaelic football – recent strikes by players, the matter of discipline and the controversy surrounding payment for players – the game is in very healthy state and it can look forward to a vibrant and exciting future.

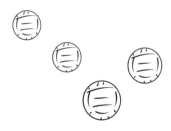

FOOTBALL GREATS

While hurling counties playing at the top-level number only about a dozen, this number could easily be doubled for football. In fact, there are few counties now that have not contested an All-Ireland Senior final. So when it comes to picking the greatest footballers of all time the task is much harder. One reason is having to pick from a larger number of players. Some of the names which crop up when the greatest footballers of all time are being discussed have never contested, never mind won, a Senior All-Ireland final. But wherever Gaelic football is played and discussed, one name is always to the fore for the title of greatest player of all time. That man is Mick O'Connell.

Mick O'Connell

Mick O'Connell was born on Valentia, an island off the Kerry coast, in 1937. Twenty-two years later, in 1959, he captained Kerry to their nineteenth All-Ireland final victory. That year Kerry did the double by also winning the National League title. O'Connell was ill on the day of the All-Ireland final, suffering from the effects of getting wet while rowing across from the island to train with the team. It was a very different era, indeed, in the history of the GAA and one the modern player would find difficult to comprehend.

Mick O'Connell was a quiet, unassuming man who let his skills on the field of play speak for him. After the All-Ireland victory in 1959 he returned home to Valentia Island that same evening, shunning the spotlight of the public's admiration and a triumphant homecoming. The next day he was back at work on the island.

But while in private he was quiet and unassuming, on the field of play he was simply majestic. He is still regarded as the finest high fielder of a ball who has ever played Gaelic football. Those who were privileged to see him soar into the air, reaching high above the hands of his opponents to safely catch the ball, will never forget it.

Kerry captain Mick O'Connell shows off his fielding skills to team trainer Dr Eamon O'Sullivan and some of his teammates in Fitzgerald Stadium during collective training before the 1959 All-Ireland. ('The Kerryman')

Football Greats

O'Connell played at a time when the catch-and-kick type of Gaelic football was popular. In this type of game, high fielders and long kickers were the princes. In an era of such men, Mick O'Connell was the undoubted king.

He played at midfield, probably the most important position in that type of game. If a team could regularly win the ball at midfield, they were guaranteed sufficient possession to go on to win the game if they had a good forward line. Good forwards were never in short supply in Kerry, the most successful football county of all time.

Mick O'Connell first came to notice aged only eighteen when he won his first county championship with South Kerry, the youngest player on that team. Within a year he was on the county Senior team and from then on his brilliance shone and his fame was guaranteed. As well as his high fielding skills, he could kick long and accurately with either foot. He could score from a long way out from goal and was also accurate with long range frees and forty-fives. He was also agile and could beat defenders with a well-timed dummy. But it was his high fielding, which brought spectators to their feet and for which he is best remembered.

Mick O'Connell's record tells of his greatness. He won four All-Ireland Senior medals, six National League medals, twelve Munster Championship medals and one Railway Cup medal. Who knows what his tally might have been had he not played in an era of two other great teams. Down burst onto the scene in 1960 and won two All-Irelands in a row before adding another in 1968. Then the finest Galway team of all time won three All-Irelands in a row between 1964 and 1966. On their way to many of those victories, either in semi-finals or finals, their opponents were Kerry.

O'Connell was named Footballer of the Year in 1962, a well-deserved honour and also won an All-Star Award in 1972. When the Team of the Century and the Team of the Millennium were chosen, Mick O'Connell rightly took his place at midfield, the greatest exponent of high fielding the game has ever seen. Like the great Christy Ring, it is said that his like will not be seen again.

Seán Purcell

Seán Purcell retired from inter-county football in 1960, just as Galway were building their finest ever football team. He began his career at the end of the 1940s when a great Mayo team were at their best and dominated in Connacht. So it is a credit to his greatness that Seán Purcell, who won just one All-Ireland Senior medal in 1956 and one National League championship in 1957, should be regarded as one of the greatest players of all time.

Seán was born in Tuam, County Galway, in 1929 and played for Tuam Stars alongside another Tuam great, Frank Stockwell. Their nickname when they played together was 'the terrible twins', an apt name for two men who terrorised the defenders they played against. In the 1956 All-Ireland final, Frank Stockwell scored 2-5, a record that still stands for a sixty-minute final. Afterwards he gave credit for his record achievement to the support he received from his fellow forward, Seán Purcell.

Sean was a versatile player and could play in any outfield position. Indeed he played in the full-back line, the half-back line and centre-field. But it was as a centre-forward that he really excelled. He was exceptionally gifted with two great feet and could kick points with either.

Football Greats

Seán Purcell.

He won six Connacht Championship medals, five of them in a row and three Railway Cup medals. He starred with St Jarlath's College in Tuam and with Tuam Stars in the County Galway championship. Because of his ability to play in almost any position on the field, many regard him as the greatest Gaelic footballer of all time. But it is as a centre-forward that he is most remembered. It was in that position that he was chosen on the Team of the Century and the Team of the Millennium, a fitting tribute to one of the greatest.

Tommy Murphy

Great GAA players are measured by their achievements on the pitch. To be included among the greats, a player should have won All-Ireland Senior honours, and National League titles. Yet one player who won neither honour, and still deserves to be called great, is Tommy Murphy, who was nicknamed 'The Boy Wonder'. The name derived from the fact that he first played Senior inter-county football for Laois when he was just sixteen years of age.

Tommy came from Graiguecullen, on the Laois–Carlow border near Carlow town. Such was his skill that he was a vital player on the Laois team that won the Leinster Championship in 1937. They lost to Kerry in the All-Ireland semi-final in a replay by just a single point. Tommy, who went off injured in that game, was thus denied an appearance in an All-Ireland final.

Laois won the Leinster Senior Championship again in 1938. In the All-Ireland semi-final of that year, Tommy Murphy was at midfield and, despite his magnificent display of high fielding, Laois again lost to Kerry. Tommy starred in many Railway Cup games and such were his abilities and style of play that spectators would go to games just to see him. He won two Railway Cup medals and also eight Laois County Championship medals with his club side, Annanough.

In 1946 Laois again won the Leinster title and played Roscommon in the All-Ireland semi-final. Roscommon had been All-Ireland champions in 1943 and 1944 and the experience stood well to them. Despite a heroic display by Tommy Murphy, Laois lost the match by two points. With that defeat went the last hope of Tommy Murphy playing for his native county in Croke Park in an All-Ireland final.

Recognised by players and spectators alike as one of the greatest players of all time, Tommy got due recognition for his talents by being chosen on the Team of the Millennium when he partnered the great Mick O'Connell at midfield. Tommy was the only player chosen on that team who had not won an All-Ireland medal.

He was also chosen on the Team of the Century, which was picked from players who had never won an All-Ireland Senior medal. In 2004, when the GAA decided to have a competition in which weaker counties knocked out of the provincial championships in early rounds would enter a secondary competition, they called it the Tommy Murphy Cup in his honour. Clare were the winners of the first ever competition and though it has fallen out of favour with many counties, it is still an honour well deserved by The Boy Wonder from Laois.

Seán O'Neill

Regarded by many as the greatest forward of his day, if not the greatest of all time, Seán O'Neill was a star before his twenty-first birthday. By the age of twenty-one he had won two All-Ireland Senior medals with Down, and would later add a third. He played in the half-forward line but he was also a deadly full-forward and scored some spectacular goals from that position.

Seán has one other claim to fame in that he was part of the Down team which was the first team from Northern Ireland to win an All-Ireland Senior title. This was in 1960 when Down beat Kerry in the final. Down were already National League champions and completed the double, as their rivals Kerry had the previous year. In 1968 Down again would achieve the double of League title and All-Ireland crown.

The team generated great excitement not only in Down but all over the country. In 1960 a record crowd of 88,000 watched them win in Croke Park. The following year the crowd rose to 91,000, the largest ever at an All-Ireland Football final. During that game they were there to witness one of the great goals of all time, scored by Seán O'Neill. As the ball rebounded off a goalpost, O'Neill somehow managed to get his boot to it and steer it into the net.

That year for his contribution to Down's success, Seán was voted Footballer of the Year. This accolade was added to his three All-Ireland Senior medals, three National League medals, six Ulster Championship medals and eight Railway Cup medals. In 1971, when the All-Star system was introduced, Seán received an All-Star Award, an honour he also received the following year. He was further honoured in 1984 when he was chosen on the Team of the Century and was also selected on the Team of the Millennium. He is still regarded as one of the greatest forwards of all time, quick, skilful and with the great forward's most striking ability – that of scoring goals. For more often than not it is goals that win games and medals and the acclamation of the crowd.

Pat Spillane

For a hurler to win eight All-Ireland medals seems an unbelievable achievement. For a footballer to do so when the competition is so much stronger and intense seems an impossibility. Yet that is the achievement of one of the greatest players – indeed probably the greatest forward of the modern era – Kerry's Pat Spillane.

He was born in Templenoe, near Kenmare, and from an early age showed great promise. At eighteen he made his Senior debut for Kerry and won a National League title. Then in 1975 came his first All-Ireland success. It was a double success for Pat that day. When the Kerry captain was injured and could not receive the Sam Maguire Cup, a nineteen-year old Pat Spillane went up the steps of the Hogan Stand to take the cup. It is a moment all young footballers dream of but few achieve and fewer still at such a young age.

Pat Spillane's tally of eight All-Ireland medals might have even been more if it was not for a great Dublin team, who won two All-Irelands in a row in 1976 and 1977, defeating Kerry in the 1976 final. Pat was also denied a medal in one of the most controversial finals of all time.

In 1982, Kerry, with Pat Spillane in fine form, met Offaly in the All-Ireland final. Kerry had won the previous four finals in a row and were going for a historic fifth win in a row, something which had never been achieved before. But a last-gasp controversial goal by Offaly's Seamus Darby robbed Kerry and Pat Spillane of further glory. But even by then his name was already written large, not only in the annals of Kerry football, but in the whole history of the GAA.

He was one of the most exciting players ever to play the game. He had great agility and could beat defenders with ease. He was extremely quick and could split a defence with a burst of speed or with a well-timed pass. He could score points with both feet from far out or near goal and was a goal poacher extraordinary.

A serious knee injury in 1983 almost put an end to his career. But in typical fashion he fought his way back to fitness and yet again starred for Kerry and won Man of the Match awards.

As well as his eight All-Ireland Senior medals, Pat won twelve Munster Championship medals, four National League titles, four Railway Cup medals and on three occasions was named Man of the Match in an All-Ireland final. He also won nine All-Star Awards, a record, which surely will stand for a long time. He retired from inter-county football in 1991 and became a contro-versial and entertaining pundit on RTÉ Television's Gaelic games programmes. The greatest accolade any sportsman can achieve is to have said of him that his like will not be seen again. That accolade can certainly be attributed to Pat Spillane.

Pat Spillane siging an autograph before the 1981 Kerry v. Offaly All-Ireland final. ('The Kerryman')

HURLING AND FOOTBALL GREATS

Teddy McCarthy

As a man who was outstanding playing both hurling and football, Teddy McCarthy holds one unique honour in the history of Gaelic games. He is the only player to win All-Ireland Senior Hurling and Football medals in the same year. He achieved this historic double in 1990 when Cork won the All-Ireland championship in both codes.

Teddy was born in Glanmire in 1965 and was part of the Cork U-21 football team that won three All-Irelands in a row between 1984 and 1986. He also won his first Senior All-Ireland Hurling medal when Cork beat Galway in the 1986 final.

In 1987 and 1988 Cork played in the All-Ireland Senior Football final but lost to Meath on each occasion. Then in 1989 Teddy won his first Senior All-Ireland Football medal when Cork beat Mayo in the final. The following year, 1990, Cork won the All-Ireland Senior Hurling final and then faced Meath in the Football final. With Teddy outstanding at midfield in that game, Cork went on to beat Meath, achieving the rare distinction of doing the double. But the greater achievement was Teddy McCarthy's double of All-Ireland Senior Football and Hurling medals in the same year.

The Story of the GAA

Teddy also won National League football and hurling medals in 1989 and 1993 respectively. He was named Footballer of the Year in 1989 and also won an All-Star Award. As few counties are capable of winning both football and hurling All-Ireland titles, it is likely that Teddy McCarthy's unique record may never be broken.

Brian Murphy

Like his fellow county player, Teddy McCarthy, Brian Murphy also holds a unique record in the annals of Gaelic games. Another of the great dual players, he is the only one to win All-Ireland medals as a Minor, U-21 and Senior player in both codes.

A noted defender, who mostly played in the full-back line, he won his All-Ireland Senior Football medal when Cork beat Galway in the 1973 final. Then between 1976 and 1978 he was part of the three-in-a-row All-Ireland winning Cork hurling team. He also won Railway Cup medals with Munster in both hurling and football and won All-Star Awards in both grades.

Jimmy Barry-Murphy

Jimmy Barry-Murphy is rightly regarded as the most exciting dual player of all time. A deadly forward in both hurling and football, he was the scourge of defenders through the 1970s and 1980s. As a goal scorer, he stands comparison with the best of all time and his goals helped Cork to glory on numerous occasions.

He made his name as a minor in both football and hurling and won his only football All-Ireland medal in 1973, scoring two goals in Cork's victory over Galway. But it was in hurling that he achieved the greater glory. He was part of the three-in-a-row Cork winning All-Ireland team of 1976–78 and added two more medals in 1984 and 1986.

His tally of medals includes three National League medals in hurling and one in football. He also holds four Railway Cup medals in football. He has been awarded seven All-Star Awards, two in football and five in hurling. He also has the distinction of winning All-Ireland Club championship medals at both hurling and football with his club, St Finbarr's. After retiring, he took up management and was manager of the Cork Senior hurling team that won the All-Ireland title in 1999.

Jimmy Barry-Murphy gets advice from the great Christy Ring during training for the 1978 final. ('Irish Examiner')

Liam Currams

Liam Currams, like Teddy McCarthy, is one of the few players to feature in All-Ireland Senior Football and Hurling finals in the same year. Currams achieved this distinction in 1981 when Offaly reached the final in both codes. Playing at midfield, Currams won his first All-Ireland Senior Hurling medal when Offaly defeated Galway in the final that year. It was a historic moment for Offaly who were winning their first All-Ireland Senior Hurling title.

Two weeks later Currams played on the Offaly senior football team in the All-Ireland final against Kerry. A strong defender in football, Currams could not prevent Kerry from winning their fourth title in a row and thus become the first player to win Senior All-Ireland Football and Hurling medals in the same year.

But the following year Offaly were back in the Senior Football final and again they faced Kerry. This time Kerry were going for their five-in-a-row sequence of wins and were denied by what is now known as the 'famous Seamus Darby goal'. But while denying Kerry history, Liam Currams was creating his own bit of history by joining an elite group of Gaelic players to win All-Ireland Senior medals in both codes. As recognition of his achievement, Currams won All-Star Awards for hurling in 1981 and for football in 1982.

Jack Lynch

Jack Lynch holds the distinction of being the most successful footballer, hurler and politician of all time, having reached the top in all three areas. He was born in 1917 and played at midfield on the Cork hurling team that won four All-Ireland Senior titles in a row between 1941 and 1944. He was captain of the 1942 team, yet another distinction.

Then in 1945 he was a forward on the Cork senior football team, which won the All-Ireland that year, defeating Cavan in the final. He was back once again in Croke Park in 1946, winning a sixth All-Ireland medal in a row when Cork beat Kilkenny in the Hurling final.

Lynch also won three National League hurling medals and three Railway Cup medals with Munster. He was chosen at midfield on the Team of the Century and on the Team of the Millennium. In his political career, he served two terms as Taoiseach in the 1960s and 1970s.

GAA COMPETITIONS IN HURLING AND FOOTBALL

The All-Ireland Senior Championship

The All-Ireland Senior Hurling and Football championships are the GAA's most prestigious competitions. They began in 1887, just three years after the founding of the association, and have been played every year since with the exception of 1888. At first club teams represented the counties, but since 1923 county teams have been picked from the best players in the county. Limerick won the first All-Ireland Football title while Tipperary won the first Hurling title.

In 1923 the Liam McCarthy Cup was introduced as the trophy for winning the All-Ireland Hurling championship. The first winners were Limerick though when they were presented with the cup in 1923, it was for winning the 1921 All-Ireland title. The 1921 championship had been delayed for two years due to the War of Independence and the Civil War. The Sam Maguire Cup for the Senior Football championship was introduced in 1928, and the first winners were Kildare.

The championship begins in May in each of the four provinces and also includes teams from London and New York. Counties in each province play each other on a knockout basis. By July the winners in each province have emerged and they now play each other in the All-Ireland semi-finals. The two winners then meet each other in Croke Park in September in the All-Ireland final, the winner being declared All-Ireland champions. In football, Kerry has been the dominant team while in hurling Cork and Kilkenny have dominated.

In 1997, the format was changed in the hurling championship. Now the beaten finalists in Munster and Leinster were allowed back into the championship. They went into a draw with Galway, the only Connacht county taking part in the Senior Championship, and the champions of Ulster. The winners of these quarter-finals now played the Leinster and Munster provincial champions in the semi-finals, the winners here going on to contest the final itself. History was made in 1997 when two teams from the same province, Clare and Tipperary from Munster, contested the All-Ireland Final, which Clare won. Offaly was the first team to actually benefit from this format change in 1998 when they won the All-Ireland title despite not having won the Leinster provincial title. There have been some changes to the back-door system since 1997, but basically it gives beaten teams a second chance.

In 2001 the GAA proposed a change to the All-Ireland Football championship and introduced what has become known as the back-door system. Under this system, teams beaten in the first round of the provincial championship go into an open draw. The four teams to emerge victorious from this phase then play the beaten finalists from the provincial championships. These four winners go on to play the provincial champions in the All-Ireland quarter-finals, with the winners contesting the semi-finals. The two winning semi-finalists then contest the All-Ireland final.

Galway was the first team to benefit from the back-door system when they won the 2001 All-Ireland title, having failed to win their provincial title. In 2003 a historic All-Ireland Football final was played between two teams from the same province. Tyrone and Armagh, both from Ulster, contested the final with Tyrone emerging winners.

The back-door system has revitalised the Football championship. It has given weaker counties another chance to take part and they have grasped the opportunity. It has meant more games and generated great excitement for the fans.

The changes to the championship formats in both hurling and football have been much criticised. But despite this criticism, the changes are the most innovative and daring the GAA has made since the championships began in 1887.

The National League

The National League began in 1926. The format has changed down through the years but still basically remains the same. Teams from the thirty-two counties and London and New York are divided into divisions. Within each division, teams play each other on a points system – two points for a win and one point each for a draw. The top teams go through to a knockout system to decide the league winners and the bottom teams are relegated.

At one time, in an effort to promote Gaelic games in America, a team from New York played the league winners in Ireland. The final in Ireland was then known as the 'home' final. In the years when New York played the 'home' final league winners, they were victorious on two occasions, in 1950 and 1966. In football, Kerry have won the most league titles while Mayo hold the record of six titles won in a row in the 1930s. In hurling Tipperary have most titles while Limerick hold the record of five titles in a row, again won in the 1930s.

In recent decades the National League suffered in popularity and prestige, as the major counties began to regard it as not being as important as winning an All-Ireland title. To remedy this, the GAA have made some changes to the format and have proposed other changes, notably linking the league to the championship. Teams relegated from their division would not be allowed to enter the back-door system once they have been knocked out in their province. Whether this will help make the league more important remains to be seen.

The Railway Cup

In the 1920s travel to sporting events in Ireland was difficult. The main means of travelling was by rail, and trains brought the bulk of the spectators to Gaelic games. In recognition of this, in 1926 the Great Southern Railway presented two cups to the GAA for an inter-provincial championship to be known as the Railway Cup.

The first championship was held in 1927 and was a huge success. The first football winners were Munster, and Leinster won the first hurling title. Both provinces have dominated the competition in hurling while Ulster and Leinster have dominated in football. Ulster holds the record for a consecutive six-in-a-row winning sequence between 1989 and 1995. (There was no competition held in 1990.)

In recent years interest in the Railway Cup has declined. This is a pity because the competition gave the top players from the lesser counties in the provinces an opportunity to play at the highest level and before a large crowd. There was also television coverage of the final and this gave people an opportunity to see some of the great players they would otherwise not have seen. In this modern age it's difficult to see how the competition can be revitalised, but it would be a pity if it ceased to be played.

The All-Ireland Minor Championship

For players under eighteen years of age, the Minor Football and Hurling championships have great importance and prestige. The Hurling championship began in 1928 with Cork emerging as winners. The Football championship began the following year with Clare, not known as a footballing county, surprisingly claiming victory.

The Minor championship is played under the same format as the Senior All-Ireland championship, and the Minor final takes place in Croke Park on All-Ireland final day. The Minor finals in both hurling and football are played just before the Senior finals.

In football, Kerry, Cork and Dublin have, unsurprisingly, won the most football titles, while in hurling Cork, Tipperary and Kilkenny, again unsurprisingly, have won most of the hurling titles.

The Under-21 Championship

This championship began in 1964 and was intended to bridge the gap between the Minor and Senior championships. In this it has been successful and many great senior players first made their mark playing at this grade. Kerry and Cork have won most U-21 titles in football and Cork also has dominated at hurling. Cork also holds one extraordinary record in the U-21 grade. In both 1970 and 1971 they won the double in hurling and football, a tremendous achievement.

The All-Ireland Club Championship

The All-Ireland Club championship began in 1971. The finals are played in Croke Park on St Patrick's Day and draw huge crowds as well as television coverage. The championship is contested by the club team that wins its county club championship. Each province has their own championship with the four winners going on to the semi-finals and the winners of that playing in the final.

It is a very important championship within the GAA. It is an opportunity for those small parishes and villages, which are the heart blood of the organisation, to have their moment of glory. It also gives players, who would never get the chance to play for their county at the top level, to represent their local area and county, and even to appear in a final in Croke Park.

Though the big clubs dominate the championship, teams from small towns and villages have gone on to win the All-Ireland Club championship. In recent times Crossmolina Deel Rovers, from a small Mayo town, have won in football while Newtownshandrum, a village in north Cork, have triumphed in hurling.

Cork teams have dominated this championship both in hurling and football with Blackrock, Glen Rovers and St Finbarr's to the fore in hurling. But in recent times they have faced stiff opposition from teams from Galway, Clare and Offaly as well as

The Story of the GAA

from Kilkenny and Tipperary. In football, Nemo Rangers from Cork along with St Finbarr's, have won the most titles. In recent years, the dominance of teams from Ulster has also been reflected in the Club football championship, especially with Crossmaglen Rangers from Armagh.

The Club championship is a very important one for the GAA and generates great local interest and passion. It is a championship where otherwise unsung heroes get a chance to shine. And while the GAA remains strong at parish level, there is little doubt but that the Club championship will continue and go from strength to strength.

Other Competitions

There are many other competitions organised by the GAA. The most important are the Nicky Rackard Cup and the Christy Ring Cup for hurling, virtually All-Ireland championships contested by the weaker counties. Football has a similar competition for the Tommy Murphy Cup. At present there is some doubt that those competitions will continue due to the reluctance of some of the weaker counties to take part.

There is also an All-Ireland Colleges championship, a Sigerson Cup competition for the universities and third level institutions, and an All-Ireland championship for vocational schools. Numerous competitions, confined to teams from each province, are also held.

CAMOGIE

The Early Years

Camogie is a version of hurling played exclusively by women. In the beginning, teams comprised twelve players but in recent times this number has been increased to fifteen. Little, if any, physical contact is allowed and shouldering, so much a part of the game of hurling, is forbidden.

Just twenty years after the founding of the GAA the first camogie clubs were formed in Dublin in 1904 and the first inter-county game was played between Dublin and Louth in 1912. Later, in 1932, specific rules were drawn up and the O'Duffy Cup was chosen as the trophy for an All-Ireland Camogie championship. This was an open draw tournament, unlike the All-Ireland Hurling championship, which is played on a provincial basis.

The O'Duffy Cup was named after Seán O'Duffy. A Mayo man, he was one of those who had fought in the 1916 Rising and was afterwards imprisoned. He was a great supporter of camogie and did much to promote the game all over the country.

The Story of the GAA

Dublin's Domination

Dublin were the first county to win the O'Duffy Cup when they became the All-Ireland Camogie champions in 1932. Cork, however, was the first team to win three titles in a row between 1939 and 1941. But it was Dublin that dominated those early years and between 1948 and 1966 they lost only one All-Ireland when Antrim won the title in 1956. One of the stars of that Dublin team was Kathleen Mills who won fifteen All-Ireland medals. It is a record that still stands and is unlikely to be broken.

Antrim won the All-Ireland once again in 1967 and Wexford won their first title in 1968 and won again in 1969. After that, the game was dominated by two teams from two of the top hurling counties, Cork and Kilkenny. Cork were the first to shine, winning four All-Irelands in a row between 1970 and 1973. That team had a star player in Marie Costine, who came from Cloyne, the same parish as Christy Ring.

Kilkenny and the Downey Sisters

The 1974 All-Ireland was won by Kilkenny, their first title. It is noted not only for that first win, but also for the appearance of a new name in camogie, that of Angela Downey. She is now regarded as the greatest player the game has ever seen. Her twin sister, Anne, also featured in that great Kilkenny team that won seven titles in a row between 1985 and 1991. Between them the Downey sisters have won an astonishing twenty-four All-Ireland medals, having both played in all those Kilkenny successes. They both also have the distinction of having captained the team to success.

The Downey sisters were born in 1957. Their father was a noted Kilkenny hurler who himself won an All-Ireland with his county in 1947. Like her father, Angela played in the forwards. She was tremendously skilful, was quick and could tear a defence apart with her devastating solo runs. Her skills helped greatly in promoting the game of camogie and increased its popularity among players and spectators alike. This rise in popularity was greatly helped by television coverage of the All-Ireland finals in which the ever-increasing skills of the camogie players could be enjoyed by a wider audience.

Cork and Tipperary's Domination

All great teams in any sport have their era and by the beginning of the 1990s Kilkenny's era came to an end. It was Cork's turn again and they won five titles in this decade. A new star, Sandie Fitzgibbon, emerged with this Cork team and drew admiration for her great abilities.

The 1990s saw the emergence of Galway, who had their first All-Ireland win in 1996. But the decade ended with the emergence of Tipperary. One of the most successful hurling counties of all time, it is odd that it took the county so long to make the breakthrough in camogie. But in typical Tipperary fashion they made their mark immediately by winning three titles in a row, their first in 1999 beating Kilkenny and adding two more titles in 2000 and 2001.

The first decade of the new millennium has been dominated by Tipperary and Cork. Only Wexford, returning to winning ways in 2007, after an absence of over thirty years, has broken the dominance of the two major teams.

Only seven counties have won All-Ireland titles. Dublin, who have not won since the 1980s, have twenty-six titles. They are followed by Cork with twenty-two, Kilkenny with twelve, Antrim with six, Tipperary with five, Wexford with four and Galway with a single title.

In recent years camogie has gone from strength to strength. There are All-Ireland championships held at almost all grades and there are also third level tournaments. An All-Star Awards system has also been introduced and a Team of the Century was chosen in 2004, honouring the great players of the previous hundred years. However, this caused great controversy when Anne Downey was omitted from the line-up.

A National League has been set up recently and this has encouraged the game in those counties where it is weak. Perhaps it will not be long before the traditional camogie counties face opposition in the All-Ireland championship from counties not usually associated with the game. This bodes well for the future of camogie and should ensure that the game continues to thrive in this new millennium.

Camogie Team of the Century

Eileen Duffy-O'Mahony, Dublin
Liz Neary, Kilkenny
Marie Costine-O'Donovan, Cork
Mary Sinnot-Dinan, Wexford
Sandy Fitzgibbon, Cork
Bridie Martin-McGarry, Kilkenny
Margaret O'Leary-Leacy, Wexford
Mairead McAtamney-Magill, Antrim
Kathleen Mills-Hill, Dublin

Camogie

Linda Mellerick, Cork
Pat Moloney-Lenihan, Cork
Una O'Connor, Dublin
Sophie Brack, Dublin
Deirdre Hughes, Tipperary
Angela Downey-Browne, Kilkenny

LADIES' GAELIC FOOTBALL

The Beginning

It is a puzzle as to why it took ninety years following the formation of the GAA for an association representing ladies' football to be set up. Though having waited so long, the first meeting to discuss the setting up of such a body was held in Hayes' Hotel in Thurles, the venue for that first meeting of Michael Cusack and his supporters at which the GAA was born.

If this venue had been chosen in the hope that ladies' football would have the success of its counterpart, then in the early years that hope was not fulfilled. Only four counties attended that first meeting – Tipperary, Galway, Kerry and Offaly – but at least there was representation from three of the four provinces.

Jim Kennedy, a Tipperary man, was elected President of what was to be known as the Ladies' Football Association. The rules of the game are somewhat similar to that of the men's game but there are some differences. Two of the most basic ones are that there is little physical contact – shouldering is not allowed – and the ball can be picked off the ground. This has led to a fast, flowing game with fewer fouls and stoppages.

In the first All-Ireland championship, only eight counties took part. These were Tipperary, Waterford, Kerry, Cork, Laois, Offaly,

Roscommon and Galway. In the first final, Tipperary defeated Offaly 2-3 to 2-2 with the game being played at Durrow, in County Laois. The 1986 All-Ireland final was played in Croke Park and has been played there ever since, attracting an ever-increasing number of spectators.

Kerry's Early Dominance

The cup for the winners of the All-Ireland championship was named the Brendan Martin Cup. Born in Tullamore, County Offaly, Brendan Martin was involved in the organisation of ladies' football in the 1970s and served as an official in the organisation. Like the Sam Maguire Cup, the Brendan Martin Cup soon found an almost permanent home in Kerry. Going many times better than their male counterparts, Kerry ladies won an incredible nine-in-a-row All-Ireland finals between 1982 and 1990.

Emergence of New Champions

Then in 1991 a new force in ladies' football came to the fore. This was Waterford, a county more noted for its hurling achievements. Between 1991 and 1995 they won four All-Ireland titles. Then new opposition emerged from Ulster: Monaghan, another team not noted for either hurling or football success, burst onto the scene and won their first title.

Waterford returned in 1998 and made the final again in 1999. They were favourites to win their second in a row but were denied by a new team to ladies' football and one that gave notice that they were here to stay. This was Mayo and they went on to win again in 2000. Going for a three-in-a-row in 2001 they were defeated by

Laois. But they returned the following year to win the first of another two-in-a-row.

But it was Cork that dominated the All-Ireland Senior championship in recent years. In 2008, when they defeated Monaghan in the final, 4-13 to 1-11, they were winning their fourth title in a row.

The Notable Players

A number of players rose to national prominence during those years and popularised the game. The most noted of these were Mary Jo Curren from Kerry, Áine Wall from Waterford, Edel Byrne from Monaghan, Sue Ramsbottom from Laois and Cora Staunton from Mayo, one of the finest forwards to play the game.

The popularity of ladies' football grew through the 1990s, largely due to the great competitive games between Waterford and Monaghan and by the advent of television coverage. The excitement caused by players like Sue Ramsbottom and Cora Staunton also raised the profile of the game. The fact that the finals were played in Croke Park also helped to create awareness that ladies' Gaelic football was a sport to be taken seriously.

Competitions and the Future

Just as in the men's game, the ladies, too, play in different age groups and there are All-Ireland championships at Minor, Junior and U-16. There is also an All-Ireland Club championship and a National League. The game has become popular among children and in secondary schools and has spread to all counties in Ireland. This interest is reflected in the large attendances for matches, especially those held in Croke Park when attendances for a ladies' final can equal or surpass important championship games in which men take part.

Though barely thirty years old, the Ladies' Football Association has made great progress. The sport is now recognised as a fine spectator sport and this is reflected in the attendances and media attention. As more counties contest the All-Ireland Senior championship, the popularity of the sport will grow accordingly and ladies' football will become an even more important part of the GAA.

Ladies' football supporters at Croke Park. (Courtesy Sportsfile II)

INTERNATIONAL RULES

Similar GAA Games

While teams from London and New York take part in the All-Ireland championships and have featured in the National League in many different formats, there has not been any real international involvement featuring teams playing Gaelic football or hurling. Probably the nearest games in similarity to Gaelic football and hurling being played outside Ireland are what are known as Australian Rules Football and shinty, a form of hurling played in Scotland.

Some matches between hurlers and shinty players from Scotland have taken place, but were more of a novelty than anything else. Shinty is a game similar to hockey and resembles the game known as hurley, which was played in Ireland at the time Michael Cusack founded the GAA. It fell into decline in Ireland when hurling, under GAA rules, became more popular. The only true international dimension in hurling and football has been in the latter, in what has become known as the Compromise Rules Series between Ireland and Australia.

Australian Rules Football does have some similarities with Gaelic football. The ball can be kicked and hand-passed. It can be caught in the hands and the player may run with it as long as he bounces it on a regular basis.

The differences are in the shape of the ball – it is oval like a rugby ball – the types of tackles allowed, which can be quite robust, and the way that scores are calculated. There is no goalkeeper and in certain circumstances when a player fields a high ball he is awarded a free kick, which is also called a 'mark'. Scores are calculated in a similar manner to the way they were calculated when the GAA was founded, with point posts being used. A goal is equivalent to six points and a ball going between the uprights and the point-posts is awarded a 'behind', the equivalent of one point.

The Compromise Rules Series

In 1984, the GAA's Centenary Year, a series of three games was organised in Ireland between an Irish team picked from the best players in the country and an Australian team. Rules, known as compromise rules, were drawn up for the games. These changed slightly as the series progressed but basically they are as follows: Goalkeepers were allowed and a goal could only be scored in a manner similar to that in Gaelic football and was worth six points. What is normally a point in Gaelic football became known as an 'over' and equivalent to three points, and a 'behind', that is a ball going between the two extra posts, counted as one point. There were other changes to the type of tackle allowed, the 'mark' was included in the game and the ball was round instead of oval.

The first series was a huge success though it was disappointing when Ireland lost by two matches to one. A problem which arose then, and which has been a major reason for the series not becoming a regular feature, was excessive physical tackling, which sometimes gave way to violent encounters between players. But despite this, a second series took place in Australia in 1986 and this time Ireland had revenge and won the series by two matches to one.

Australia came to Ireland a second time in 1987 and again emerged as the winners. But Ireland had revenge once more on their next visit to Australia in 1988. This was to be the last series of matches between the two countries until 1998. On this occasion Ireland became the first of the two countries to win a home test and they won again the following year in Australia. But since then Australia have won five series to Ireland's three.

Since 2004, the cup presented to the winners of the series is known as the Cormac MacAnallen Cup. It is named in honour of the Tyrone footballer who died in 2004 from a heart condition, and who had played for Ireland against Australia.

Australia were the first winners of this trophy and they retained the trophy in 2006. Because of violence during the 2006 series, it seemed as if the competition was doomed and would not be played again.

But after talks between the GAA and the Australian Rules organisers, it was decided to play another series in Australia in 2008. This was a huge success and the two games that were played were both close and exciting with Ireland emerging as the winners and receiving the Cormac MacAnallen Cup for the first time. The games were played in a sporting manner and there was no violence and it was decided to continue the series in Ireland in 2009.

A negative aspect of the series, though, has been the loss of some of our own Gaelic players to the Australian game. Jim Stynes from Dublin, Tadgh Kenneally from Kerry and Setanta Ó hAilpín from Cork are the best known of these and they have enjoyed great success in Australia. But their loss to the Irish game has caused some worry within the GAA and there are fears that more players may go to Australia, where the game is played professionally and where players can earn a good living. In the coming years we may see more players going to Australia to the detriment of the game here.

But overall, the series has been a success. It has given an opportunity for some of the best GAA footballers of recent years to represent their country at international level. The games have drawn large crowds and when played in a sporting manner have created great spectacle. It seems that the future of the Compromise Rules Series is assured.

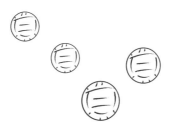

HANDBALL

The Beginning

There are references to the game of handball dating back to the eighteenth century. But it was not until 1923 that the GAA became officially involved in the sport. And while often regarded as the GAA's least important sport, nevertheless handball has a special place in the history of Gaelic games. It is the only true international sport that is administered by the association. In times gone by, a ball alley was often the only sporting facility a small village or parish might possess, and was a focal point and gathering place for young people.

There are many variations of the game and of the type of ball used and of the structure and size of the ball alley, but the game itself is quite basic. It is similar to squash except the players – two in a single's game and four in a double's game – use their hands to strike the ball rather than using rackets as in squash. The server can score points each time he causes his opponent to fail to return a ball and the first person to twenty-one points wins the game or set. A match usually consists of three sets and the best of three sets wins the match.

The GAA did much to promote handball when in 1923 they oversaw the setting up of provincial handball councils. In 1924 the

Handball

Irish Handball Council was established, an independent body intended to promote the game but remaining part of the GAA. In 1925 the first All-Ireland championships were held. As in other GAA sports some counties excelled more than others and two counties with a long tradition in the game are Roscommon and Kilkenny. Both had star players in those early years in Pat Perry of Roscommon and J. J. Gilmartin of Kilkenny.

The International Game

Right from the early days of the GAA handball was played internationally. It was popular in the United States, Canada, Australia, Spain and Mexico and is still played in those countries. In the United States a smaller ball alley was used and this was introduced into Ireland in the 1970s. It had one important difference from the ball alleys already in existence – it was fully enclosed and the roof was used as a fifth wall. Having a roof meant that the game could be played in all weathers, an important point in a country where the weather can often be both cold and wet. To reflect this new interest in handball, an alley was built in Croke Park in 1970. In that year the World Handball Championships were held at the stadium.

This new game in the enclosed court gained popularity. This was helped by the support received from RTÉ with its 'Top Ace' programme. Stars to emerge from this era were Peadar McGee from Mayo, Pat Kirby of Clare, another strong handball county, and Jimmy Goggins and Dick Lyng of Wexford.

Michael 'Duxie' Walsh

But it was in the 1980s that the greatest Irish player of all time emerged. This man was Michael 'Duxie' Walsh from Kilkenny and he had no equal. His record of thirteen singles titles in a row in the older type of game and seven in a row in the more modern game show his complete dominance of the sport. He also excelled in doubles when he was partnered by no other than the finest hurler of the modern game, and also a Kilkenny man, the great D. J. Carey.

Irish World Champions

The man regarded as the finest Irish handball player today is Paul Brady from Cavan. He has the distinction of beating 'Duxie' Walsh in the Irish championships and is the first Irishman to win a world singles title, which he won in 2003. Another Irish player of note is Tony Healy from Cork.

Women also play handball and created their own piece of history when in 2003 Fiona Shannon from County Antrim won the women's singles title in the World Handball Championships.

In recent years the popularity of handball has waned. This is probably due to the increasing number of other sports now being played in Ireland. The lack of media and television coverage has also contributed to this decline. But on the international stage handball still thrives, especially in the United States and Canada and may one day regain the popularity it once held in Ireland.

GREAT GAA FAMILIES

The Donnellans, Galway

The Donnellan family from Dunmore, County Galway, is the most famous of all Galway GAA families. Mick Donnellan first came to prominence when he won an All-Ireland senior football medal with Galway in the controversial All-Ireland Championship of 1925.

That year, there were numerous drawn games in Connacht and, because of this, the Connacht final was delayed for months. The GAA nominated Mayo to play in the All-Ireland Championship and Mayo emerged as winners. But then Mayo were ordered to play Galway in the Connacht final, a match which Galway won. Galway were then controversially declared All-Ireland Champions, giving John Donnellan his medal. He later captained Galway in the 1933 All-Ireland final when they were beaten by Cavan.

In the 1960s Mick's two sons, Pat and John both played for Galway. This was the great era for Galway football when they won their famous three-in-a-row All-Ireland Senior crowns. John was the Galway captain in 1964 when they won the first of their three-in-a-row, beating Kerry. During that game Mick Donnellan, who was watching from the Hogan Stand, died of a heart attack. It was a very sad and tragic happening on what should have been a great day for the family.

The following year Pat Donnellan was at midfield for Galway while John as usual played in the defence. Galway was again triumphant and they repeated the win in 1966 to complete the three-in-a-row. The brothers also won National League medals in 1965 and featured on the Connacht Railway Cup winning team of 1967.

John Donnellan's son, Michael, would continue the family success more than thirty years after the great three-in-a-row was achieved. With Michael in terrific form, Galway beat Kildare in 1998 to be crowned All-Ireland champions. As recognition of his contribution, he won an All-Star Award and was also named Footballer of the Year.

Galway were back in Croke Park in 2000 but lost in the final to Kerry. The following year they were back again, this time defeating Meath to give Michael Donnellan his second All-Ireland medal.

The Larkins, Kilkenny

Like the Donnellan family, the Larkin family of Kilkenny hold the distinction of having three generations of All-Ireland winners in hurling. Paddy was the first member of the family to see success, winning four All-Ireland Hurling medals in 1932, '33, '35 and '36.

In 1963, his son, Philip Larkin, better known by his nickname 'Fan', won his first Senior medal. In the 1970s he went on to win four more Senior medals in 1972, '74, '75 and '79. He also won five Railway Cup medals in the 1970s and in 1976 was Kilkenny's captain when they won the National League title. A noted defender, he was also the recipient of four All-Star Awards.

Fan's son, Philip, continued the family tradition of winning All-Ireland Hurling medals with Kilkenny. A noted defender like his father, he won his first Senior medal in 2000 and won two in row in 2002 and 2003.

The Ó Sés, Kerry

The Ó Sé family come from Ventry, County Kerry. The first member of note was Páidí who, along with Pat Spillane, won eight All-Ireland Senior Football medals in that great era of Kerry dominance in the 1970s and 1980s. He was one of the finest defenders ever to play football and won a total of five All-Star Awards between 1981 and 1985. In 1985 he captained Kerry to All-Ireland victory over Dublin.

In 1996 Páidí was appointed Kerry manager. Kerry won the Munster Championship that year but lost in the All-Ireland semi-final to Mayo. The following year they had revenge on Mayo when they beat them in the All-Ireland final. Darragh and Tomás Ó Sé, Páidí's nephews, were on the team, which earlier that year had also won the National League title. Páidí now joined a small group of footballers who had won All-Ireland Senior titles as a player and a manager.

In 2000 Kerry again won the All-Ireland with Páidí as manager and with both Darragh and Tomás on the team.

Páidí Ó Sé, captain of the 1985 All-Ireland winning team. (Sportsfile)

Kerry were beaten in the 2002 All-Ireland final by Armagh but came back to win again in 2004, though Darragh did not play because he was injured. Then in 2006, joined by brother Marc, three Ó Sé brothers played on the Kerry team which beat Mayo. In doing so they joined an elite band of brothers who had won All-Ireland honours on the same team on the same day. This was a feat they repeated in 2007 when again Kerry were crowned All-Ireland champions, beating Cork in the first all-Munster All-Ireland Football final.

The Hendersons, Kilkenny

The Henderson brothers, Pat, Ger and John, came from Johnstown and between them won almost every honour in the game of hurling. Pat, the eldest, was born in 1943 and was one of the finest centre-backs of his era. He won his first All-Ireland Senior Hurling medal in 1967 when Kilkenny beat old rivals, Tipperary in the final. He also won Senior medals in 1969, '72, '74 and '75, as well as two National League medals in 1966 and 1976. He added six Railway Cup medals to this tally, won two All-Star Awards and in 1974 was voted Hurler of the Year.

Ger Henderson, who also played in the centre-backs, replaced his brother Pat on the Kilkenny team and won three All-Ireland Senior medals in 1979, '82 and '83. He added two National League titles to this tally as well as a Railway Cup medal. He won a total of five All-Star Awards and like his brother Pat, was voted Hurler of the Year, his honour coming in 1979.

John won All-Ireland Senior medals in the same year as his brother Ger and added four National League titles to this tally. Like both his older brothers, he also won an All-Star Award in

1983, making the Hendersons only the second family of three brothers to win All-Star Awards in hurling, the other winners being the Dooley brothers from Offaly. Between them the three Henderson brothers won a total of eleven All-Ireland Senior medals, making them one of the most noted families in the annals of hurling.

The Spillanes, Kerry

Kerry has produced some great footballers and some great football families but the most successful of them all has to be the Spillane brothers, Pat, Mick and Tom. Between them, they won nineteen All-Ireland Senior medals and were stars in a Kerry team of stars that dominated Gaelic football in the mid-1970s and early 1980s.

Pat was the most famous of the three brothers and won a grand total of eight All-Ireland Senior medals, including four in a row and three in a row. He also holds the record of nine All-Star Awards, eight in the same position of left half-forward. He also holds four National League medals and four Railway Cup medals and was twice voted Footballer of the Year, in 1978 and 1986. He was one of the most exciting forwards ever to play Gaelic football and was a deadly finisher.

Pat's brother, Mick Spillane, was a defender of great ability and won seven All-Ireland medals, and was part of the Kerry team that won four-in-a-row and three-in-a-row All-Ireland titles between 1978 and 1986. His excellence as a defender was recognised in 1985 when he won an All-Star Award.

The youngest of the three brothers was Tom Spillane. He was part of the three-in-a-row winning Kerry team of 1984–86 and won his first Senior medal as a sub in 1981. He also picked up three All-Star Awards: in 1984, 1986 and 1987. He was a versatile player who could play in defence or attack but won most of his acclaim as Kerry's centre-back. The Spillane brothers are the only set of three brothers who have all won All-Star Football Awards, a fitting honour for one of the finest Gaelic football families of all time.

FAMOUS GAA GROUNDS

Croke Park, Dublin

The name Croke Park, known worldwide among Irish people, is associated with sporting prowess, fame, glamour, joy and success. Even the names for particular parts of the grounds – Hogan Stand, Cusack Stand, Hill 16, the Canal End and the Railway End – are steeped in the memories of Irish people.

The magnificent stadium we know today, one of the finest in Europe, was at the time of the founding of the GAA in 1884 an area of green grass. It was then known as the City and Suburban Sports' Grounds, or more commonly called Jones' Road.

In the early days the GAA hired the ground for events, the first of which, an athletics meeting, took place on 10 September 1891. It was not until 1896 that the first Gaelic games were played there. On 15 March that year, Tipperary, represented by Arravale Rovers, defeated Meath's Pierce O'Mahonys 0-4 to 0-3 in what was the final of the 1895 All-Ireland Football championship. On the same day, Tipperary won the All-Ireland Hurling title when Tubberadora beat Tullyroan of Kilkenny 6-8 to 1-0.

In 1907 Jones' Road was put up for sale. The GAA did not have enough money to buy the ground and a Limerick man, Frank

Dineen, bought it. He had been a noted athlete and was a GAA supporter. He realised that the GAA needed a proper stadium and it was for this reason he bought the ground.

He made many improvements and rented the ground to the GAA for events. Then in 1913, after organising a tournament, the Croke Cup, in honour of their patron, Archbishop Croke, who had died in 1902, the GAA was able to buy Jones' Road from Dineen. As a further tribute to Archbishop Croke, they named the ground in his honour.

An aerial view of Croke Park. (Courtesy Sportsfile II)

On 2 November 1913, Kilkenny beat Tipperary in the All-Ireland Hurling final. Then, on 14 December 1913, Kerry beat Wexford in the All-Ireland Football final. These were the first finals to be played at the newly named Croke Park. Since then, the stadium has hosted almost all of the finals, with three exceptions. The first was in 1937 when, due to work at the ground, the All-Ireland Hurling final was played in Killarney. In 1947 the All-Ireland Football final was played at the Polo Grounds in New York. Then, in 1984, the Centenary All-Ireland Hurling final was played at Semple Stadium, Thurles, to mark the founding of the GAA in that town.

Down through the years the stadium has seen many changes. After the 1916 Easter Rising, Hill 16 was constructed from the rubble of the shelled buildings in Dublin. Then in 1926 the newly erected Hogan Stand was named after Michael Hogan who was killed by the Black and Tans on Bloody Sunday. The Cusack Stand was completed in 1938 and named in honour of the founder of the GAA. The terrace at the Canal End opened in 1950 and two years later the Nally Stand honoured the name of Mayo athlete Padraig Nally.

Croke Park has witnessed many historic moments. In 1926 the first radio broadcast of a field game in Europe took place from the stadium. Before that, only in the USA had a field game been broadcast on radio. In 1970 the World Handball Championships were held at the stadium. In 1972, Muhammad Ali, the greatest heavyweight boxer in the history of the sport, fought in Croke Park. Then, in 1984, the first games in what were to be known as the International Rules Series between Australia and Ireland were held there. In 2003 the opening and closing ceremonies for the Special Olympics were held in the stadium. More history was created when the stadium was opened for both soccer and rugby internationals in 2007 and also in that year the first floodlit match took place.

In 1990 a development plan for Croke Park was proposed. This saw the demolition of the old stands and new ones erected. Hill 16 was also redeveloped and the stadium now has a capacity of just over 82,000.

Today, Croke Park is a fitting headquarters and stadium for the GAA and also houses the GAA museum. It is rightly regarded as one of the finest sports grounds in Europe, if not in the whole world. It is a powerful reminder of the achievements of the GAA and of the dreams of men like Michael Cusack and Frank Dineen and of the hundreds of thousands of GAA players and supporters in every corner of the globe.

Semple Stadium, Thurles

Semple Stadium in Thurles, County Tipperary, is the second most famous and important GAA ground in Ireland. With a capacity of 53,500, it is the second largest stadium in the country and is rightly renowned for its excellent playing surface.

The original ground on which the stadium stands was purchased in 1910 for £900. In 1934 improvements were made to the original grounds, which were held in trust until 1956 when they were handed over to the GAA. Further improvements were made in 1968.

In 1971 the stadium was named Semple Stadium after Thomas Semple, who came from Thurles. He was captain of the Thurles Blues and won All-Ireland Senior Hurling medals in 1900, 1906 and 1908. The stadium's most famous honour came in 1984 when the Centenary All-Ireland Senior Hurling final between Cork and Offaly was played there. It was a fitting tribute to Thurles where, 100 years before, the GAA was founded.

Famous GAA Grounds

Páirc Úí Chaoimh, Cork

Páirc Úí Chaoimh is built on what was originally the Cork Athletic Grounds. The area had been used for GAA events from around 1890. In 1904 the Cork Athletic Grounds opened on the site and staged the delayed 1902 All-Ireland finals there. Down through the years the ground became famous for hosting some of the finest Munster Hurling finals ever seen.

In 1974 a new stadium was built. It was named after Pádraig Ó Caoimh, who was general secretary of the GAA from 1929 to 1964. He was born in Roscommon but lived most of his life in Cork. He is credited with being one of the most important GAA administrators of all time.

The stadium was opened in June 1976. On that day Cork hurlers played Kilkenny and the footballers played Kerry. The stadium has a capacity of nearly 50,000 and at present there are plans to develop it further.

St Tiernach's Park, Clones

The ground was bought by the GAA in 1944 for £700 and was named after a local saint. It was officially opened on 6 August of that year. In the 1990s it was redeveloped and the famous bank, which gave the ground its unique look and atmosphere, was removed and replaced with seating. Opposite this, a new stand was also erected.

Clones, as it is most usually known, is now the premier GAA stadium in Ulster. Since the 1970s it has hosted the Ulster Senior Football Championship final, as well as other important matches. But between 2004 and 2006 and Ulster Senior Football final was played in Croke Park. This was due to the huge increase in interest in football in Ulster due to the dominance of teams from that province in the All-Ireland championship. This in turn led to a huge increase in the number of spectators wishing to see the final and Clones, with its capacity of around 36,000 could not cope with the demand. The 2007 Ulster final, however, was held in Clones and at the moment there is talk of developing the ground further.

Dr Hyde Park, Roscommon

Known in the past as Rafferty's Field, the stadium now named Dr Hyde Park hosted GAA matches since the 1930s. Then in 1969 it was purchased and named after the first President of Ireland, who was born in County Roscommon.

The first Connacht championship match was held there in 1971 and afterwards the venue was used extensively with some famous Connacht Championship matches being staged there, none more thrilling than the 1989 final between Mayo and Roscommon, which went to extra time and in which Mayo emerged triumphant.

In the 1990s the ground was redeveloped and a new stand built. The capacity is now around 30,000 and it is one of the finest grounds in Connacht.

McHale Park, Castlebar

McHale Park in Castlebar, County Mayo, is the home of Castlebar Mitchels football club. The original land was purchased in 1930 for around £650 and the newly built stadium was officially opened on 24 May 1931. It was named after John McHale, who was Archbishop of the Tuam diocese between 1834 and 1881.

The ground was redeveloped between 1950 and 1952 and the capacity increased to around 40,000. Then, in 1980, covered seating was provided. Again in the 1990s there was much redevelopment including new dressing rooms and other facilities. At present McHale Park has a capacity of around 36,000 and there are plans in the pipeline to further increase this number in the coming years.

Fitzgerald Stadium, Killarney

Without doubt, Fitzgerald Stadium in Killarney is one of the most beautiful sporting venues in all of Ireland. It is named after one of Kerry's most famous footballers, Dick Fitzgerald. He won five All-Ireland Senior Football medals and was captain of the Kerry team, which won All-Irelands in 1913 and 1914.

The original ground was bought by the Kerry GAA in the 1930s and it was officially opened on 31 May 1936 when Kerry played Mayo. The stadium has hosted some of the finest Munster football finals of all time and is a noted venue for great matches between rival neighbours Cork and Kerry.

It has also been used extensively for Munster hurling finals and has seen great rivals Tipperary and Cork challenge for supremacy in Munster on many occasions. In 1937 Fitzgerald Stadium hosted the All-Ireland Hurling final in which Tipperary easily beat their great rivals, Kilkenny. In recent years the ground has been improved and is now one of the finest in Munster. But it is its setting at the foot of the MacGillicuddy's Reeks that sets Fitzgerald Stadium apart from all the other GAA grounds in Ireland.

FAMOUS GAA PEOPLE

Michael Cusack

Michael Cusack, the founder of the GAA was born in Carron, County Clare, on 20 September 1847. He came from an Irish-speaking family and trained as a teacher. In 1874 he became a professor in Blackrock College in Dublin and three years later started his own school which became known as Cusack's Academy.

He was a noted athlete, especially in throwing weights and shot-putting and was an All-Ireland champion. As a young man he had seen the game of hurling played in his native county and wished to ensure that it survived. With this aim in mind, when he moved to Dublin he set up the Dublin Hurling Club where he hoped to combine the two forms of hurling then being played in Ireland. But disputes arose between players from both forms of the game and the club disbanded.

Following this setback, Cusack set up the Dublin Metropolitan Hurling Club, which concentrated on the game of hurling we know today. He organised matches with other clubs and began to draw up rules for the game.

Cusack was also passionately interested in athletics and was involved with a number of athletic clubs in Dublin where he took part in the events. But he became disillusioned with the organisation of athletics in Ireland and especially with the Amateur Athletic Association (AAA), which governed the sport. This was an English-based organisation. It did not fully support what Cusack saw as Irish pastimes and was reluctant to allow ordinary Irish athletes to take part in events. It was also corrupt and favoured certain athletes over others.

Cusack realised that what was needed was a new organisation to oversee athletics in Ireland. This organisation would support Irish pastimes and ordinary Irish athletes and would treat everyone fairly.

With this aim in mind Cusack called the famous meeting in Hayes' Hotel in Thurles on 1 November 1884. It was at this meeting that the GAA was set up and Cusack was appointed its secretary. The newly formed association had almost immediate success and was to go on to be the most importing sporting organisation in Ireland.

However, for Michael Cusack, his position of secretary of the GAA was short-lived. He was a difficult man to get on with and angered many other members of the GAA with his behaviour. Within two years he had lost his post as secretary and afterwards played no further part in the GAA. Despite this, his founding of the GAA would guarantee him a unique place in the world of Gaelic games and he has had many honours bestowed on him, the most notable being that of the naming of the Cusack Stand in Croke Park after him. The house where he was born in Carron has now been restored and is a museum to his memory.

Michael Cusack died on 28 November 1906 and was buried in Glasnevin Cemetery in Dublin. He had a short association with the GAA but his legacy lives on in the success of the organisation, which he founded that November day in 1884.

Sam Maguire

The name of Sam Maguire is probably the most famous in the history of the GAA. A Corkman, Sam was born outside the town of Dunmanway in 1888. Like many boys from a farming community, he went to work in London. There he played football with the Hibernian Club. He played in three All-Ireland finals with Hibernians but was never on a winning side.

Sam had a great love of Ireland, its language, music and pastimes. He was a staunch supporter of the GAA and when he stopped playing became involved in the administration of the GAA in London. He was also a Republican and a member of the IRB, a secret organisation determined to win Ireland her freedom from England. It was Maguire who swore in Michael Collins as a member of the IRB. Later Collins would win freedom for twenty-six counties in Ireland in what became known as the War of Independence.

When Ireland got her independence, Sam Maguire returned to Dublin to work in the General Post Office. When his great friend Michael Collins was killed, Maguire became disillusioned with Ireland. He was eventually sacked from his job and died in near poverty in 1927.

After his death some friends decided that his name should not be forgotten and had a silver cup designed in his honour. It was made to resemble the Ardagh Chalice, an ancient chalice found buried in County Limerick some years before. The cup was named the Sam Maguire Cup and from 1928 on it has been presented to the winning captain of the All-Ireland Football championship. Willie Gannon from Kildare was the first man to receive the cup.

A new Sam Maguire Cup was made for the All-Ireland final of 1988. Meath were the first winners when they defeated Cork in the final. The first man to receive the new cup was Joe Cassells, the Meath captain. The old cup can now be seen in the GAA museum in Croke Park.

Sam Maguire is buried in the Church of Ireland churchyard in Dunmanway. A Celtic cross marks his grave. A statue in his honour also stands in the square in the town, another tribute to a famous local man whose name will never be forgotten.

Liam McCarthy

Liam McCarthy was born in England of Irish parents. Like Sam Maguire, he had a great love of all things Irish. He was a staunch GAA supporter in London and had a particular love of hurling. He was very impressed with the work being done by the GAA and decided to give the organisation a cup in recognition of this.

The cup was named the Liam McCarthy Cup in his honour. It soon became the most important trophy in hurling, being the cup presented each year since 1923 to the captain of the All-Ireland Hurling champions in Croke Park. Though first presented in 1923 to R. McConkey, the captain of the victorious Limerick hurling team, that match was actually the final of the 1921 All-Ireland Hurling championship, which had had to be postponed for two years due to war in Ireland.

The Liam McCarthy Cup eventually had to be replaced and this was done in 1992. Kilkenny were the first winners of the new trophy when they defeated Cork in the final. Kilkenny captain

Liam Fennelly received the cup in Croke Park on 6 September that year. The old cup, like the Sam Maguire Cup, can now be seen in the GAA museum.

Micheál O'Hehir

Like the founder of the GAA, Micheál O'Hehir was a Clareman. The family were staunch GAA supporters and his father, Jim O'Hehir, trained the team from Quin, which won Clare's first All-Ireland title in 1914.

Micheál began his career as a commentator for Radio Éireann in 1938 while still a teenager. His first game was the All-Ireland Football semi-final between Galway and Monaghan. After that he was to become the recognised voice of the GAA. In times when it was difficult to travel to see matches, and there was no television coverage, O'Hehir brought the atmosphere and excitement of the games to a wide audience.

In those long gone times, few people possessed radios and it was common for people from the surrounding area to gather in a house that had a radio on a Sunday afternoon to listen to the commentary on the games. It has often been said that the best way to 'see' a GAA game was to listen to Micheál O'Hehir's radio commentary.

He commentated on ninety-nine All-Ireland Hurling and Football finals but his most famous broadcast was the 1947 All-Ireland Football final, played in New York. Micheál brought all the excitement of the match to hundreds of thousands of people in Ireland and when it seemed that the link between Ireland and New York would be cut before the game was over, he pleaded to be given a few more minutes. He was given the few minutes and completed the commentary.

Micheál O'Hehir. (Courtesy Connolly Collection)

When television coverage of GAA matches began, Micheál proved himself up to the task. Once again his commentary added to the excitement and enjoyment of the matches. On the eve of his 100th All-Ireland commentary, he was taken ill and never again commentated on a match. But he is still fondly remembered by those who heard his commentaries, and has no rival for the claim to have been the 'voice of the GAA' for fifty years.

The Story of the GAA

Sean Lavan

One of the most exciting moments in any Gaelic football match is when a player goes on a solo run. Anyone who has seen Pat Spillane of Kerry streaking through a defence at speed before smashing the ball into the net will never forget the moment. This most exciting and effective skill, also described as toe-to-hand, was first used by Mayo man, Sean Lavan.

Sean Lavan was born in Kiltimagh in 1898 and at first was a schoolteacher. As well as being a noted footballer, he was also a fine athlete and held many Irish athletic titles. He also represented Ireland in two Olympic Games.

The rules of Gaelic football state that a player may take no more then four steps while holding the ball in his hands. It was to get around this restriction of not being allowed to run with the ball that Sean Lavan invented the solo run. By dropping the ball from the hands and tapping it back into the hands using the toe of the boot, a player could race forward without causing an infringement of the rules.

It is claimed that Sean made his first solo run with the ball during a match between Mayo and Dublin in 1921. Though it is claimed that he did score a point at the end of the run, the referee disallowed the score. But the solo run was born and would become part of Gaelic football.

Sean Lavan gave up teaching and later trained as a doctor. He died in 1973 and, thanks to the solo run, his name still lives on in the annals of Gaelic games. His contribution to Gaelic football is one of the most exciting innovations the game has ever seen. It is one of the skills to have brought fame to many players and thrills and excitement to those who love the game and who go to watch it.

Micheál Ó Muircheartaigh

Micheál Ó Muircheartaigh is a Kerryman, and is rightly regarded as the second most important GAA commentator of all time. He was born near Dingle in 1930 and, like Micheál O'Hehir, he built his reputation in radio and became a noted commentator in the Irish language. His first broadcast was in Irish in the 1949 Railway Cup final.

His accent is unique and he could never be mistaken for anyone else. He has an encyclopaedic knowledge of the GAA and of the people involved, and one of the joys of his commentaries is his imparting of this knowledge, which he seamlessly weaves into the action.

Like Micheál O'Hehir, he can create pictures of the game in a listener's head and can even make the most unexciting game appear like a classic. In the days before Irish people in other parts of the world had access to television coverage of games, Micheál Ó Muircheartaigh brought the excitement of GAA matches to them in his unique and inimitable style. Now nearing his eighties, he still commentates on GAA matches and has lost none of his enthusiasm for the games he so obviously loves.

COUNTY COLOURS

Antrim:	Saffron and white
Armagh:	Orange
Carlow:	Red, green and yellow
Cavan:	Royal blue
Clare:	Saffron and blue
Cork:	Red
Derry:	White with red hoop
Donegal:	Green and gold
Down:	Red and black
Dublin:	Blue with navy cuffs
Fermanagh:	Green and white
Galway:	Maroon and white
Kerry:	Green with gold hoops
Kildare:	White
Kilkenny:	Black and amber stripes
Laois:	Blue with white hoop
Leitrim:	Green with gold hoop
Limerick:	Green with white cuffs
Longford:	Blue and gold
Louth:	Red
Mayo:	Green with red hoop

County Colours

Meath:	Green
Monaghan:	White with blue collar and cuffs
Offaly:	Green, white and orange hoops
Roscommon:	Yellow with blue cuffs
Sligo:	White with black cuffs and collar
Tipperary:	Blue with gold hoops
Tyrone:	White with red cuffs and collar
Waterford:	White
Westmeath:	Maroon and white
Wexford:	Gold with purple top
Wicklow:	Blue with gold hoop

FACTS AND FIGURES

ALL-IRELAND SENIOR HURLING WINNERS

1887:   Tipperary 1-1, Galway 0-0
1888:   No competition held
1889:   Dublin 5-1, Clare 1-6
1890:   Cork 1-6, Wexford 2-2 (Cork declared winners)
1891:   Kerry 2-3, Wexford 1-5
1892:   Cork 2-4, Dublin 1-1
1893:   Cork 6-8, Kilkenny 0-2
1894:   Cork 5-20, Dublin 2-0
1895:   Tipperary 6-8, Kilkenny 1-0
1896:   Tipperary 8-14, Dublin 0-4
1897:   Limerick 3-4, Kilkenny 2-4
1898:   Tipperary 7-13, Kilkenny 3-10
1899:   Tipperary 3-12, Wexford 1-4
1900:   Tipperary 2-5, London 0-6
1901:   London 1-5, Cork 0-4
1902:   Cork 2-13, London 0-0
1903:   Cork 3-16, London 1-1
1904:   Kilkenny 1-9, Cork 1-8
1905:   Cork 5-10, Kilkenny 3-13 (Replay ordered)
Replay: Kilkenny 7-7, Cork 2-9
1906:   Tipperary 3-16, Dublin 3-8
1907:   Kilkenny 3-12, Cork 3-8

1908:   Tipperary 2-5, Dublin 1-8 (Draw)
Replay: Tipperary 3-15, Dublin 1-5
1909:   Kilkenny 4-6, Tipperary 0-12
1910:   Wexford 7-0, Limerick 6-2
1911:   Kilkenny 3-3, Tipperary 2-1
1912:   Kilkenny 2-1, Cork 1-3
1913:   Kilkenny 2-4, Tipperary 1-2
1914:   Clare 5-1, Laois 1-0
1915:   Laois 6-2, Cork 4-1
1916:   Tipperary 5-4, Kilkenny 3-2
1917:   Dublin 5-4, Tipperary 4-2
1918:   Limerick 9-5, Wexford 1-3
1919:   Cork 6-4, Dublin 2-4
1920:   Dublin 4-9, Cork 4-3
1921:   Limerick 8-5, Dublin 3-2
1922:   Kilkenny 4-2, Tipperary 2-6
1923:   Galway 7-3, Limerick 4-5
1924:   Dublin 5-3, Galway 2-6
1925:   Tipperary 5-6, Galway 1-5
1926:   Cork 4-6, Kilkenny 2-0
1927:   Dublin 4-8, Cork 1-3
1928:   Cork 6-12, Galway 1-0
1929:   Cork 4-9, Galway 1-3
1930:   Tipperary 2-7, Dublin 1-3
1931:   Cork 1-6, Kilkenny 1-6 (Draw)
Replay: Cork 5-8, Kilkenny 3-4
1932:   Kilkenny 3-3, Clare 2-3
1933:   Kilkenny 1-7, Limerick 0-6
1934:   Limerick 2-7, Dublin 3-4 (Draw)
Replay: Limerick 5-2, Dublin 2-6
1935:   Kilkenny 2-5, Limerick 2-4

1936: Limerick 5-6, Kilkenny 1-5

1937: Tipperary 3-11, Kilkenny 0-3

1938: Dublin 2-5, Waterford 1-6

1939: Kilkenny 2-7, Cork 3-3

1940: Limerick 3-7, Kilkenny 1-7

1941: Cork 5-11, Dublin 0-6

1942: Cork 2-14, Dublin 3-4

1943: Cork 5-16, Antrim 0-4

1944: Cork 2-13, Dublin 1-2

1945: Tipperary 5-6, Kilkenny 3-6

1946: Cork 7-5, Kilkenny 3-8

1947: Kilkenny 0-14, Cork 2-7

1948: Waterford 6-7, Dublin 4-2

1949: Tipperary 3-11, Laois 0-3

1950: Tipperary 1-9, Kilkenny 1-8

1951: Tipperary 7-7, Wexford 3-9

1952: Cork 2-14, Dublin 0-7

1953: Cork 3-3, Galway 0-8

1954: Cork 1-9, Wexford 1-6

1955: Wexford 3-13, Galway 2-8

1956: Wexford 2-14, Cork 2-8

1957: Kilkenny 4-10, Waterford 3-12

1958: Tipperary 4-9, Galway 2-5

1959: Waterford 1-17, Kilkenny 5-5 (Draw)

Replay: Waterford 3-12, Kilkenny 1-10

1960: Wexford 2-15, Tipperary 0-11

1961: Tipperary 0-16, Dublin 1-12

1962: Tipperary 3-10, Wexford 2-11

1963: Kilkenny 4-17, Waterford 6-8

1964: Tipperary 5-13, Kilkenny 2-8

1965: Tipperary 2-16, Wexford 0-10

Facts and Figures

1966:   Cork 3-9, Kilkenny 1-10

1967:   Kilkenny 3-8, Tipperary 2-7

1968:   Wexford 5-8, Tipperary 3-12

1969:   Kilkenny 2-15, Cork 2-9

1970:   Cork 6-21, Wexford 5-10

1971:   Tipperary 5-17, Kilkenny 5-14

1972:   Kilkenny 3-24, Cork 5-11

1973:   Limerick 1-21, Kilkenny 1-14

1974:   Kilkenny 3-19, Limerick 1-13

1975:   Kilkenny 2-22, Galway 2-10

1976:   Cork 2-21, Wexford 4-11

1977:   Cork 1-17, Wexford 3-8

1978:   Cork 1-15, Kilkenny 2-8

1979:   Kilkenny 2-12, Galway 1-8

1980:   Galway 2-15, Limerick 3-9

1981:   Offaly 2-12, Galway 0-15

1982:   Kilkenny 3-18, Cork 1-13

1983:   Kilkenny 2-14, Cork 2-12

1984:   Cork 3-16, Offaly 1-12

1985:   Offaly 2-11, Galway 1-12

1986:   Cork 4-12, Galway 2-15

1987:   Galway 1-12, Kilkenny 0-9

1988:   Galway 1-15, Tipperary 0-14

1989:   Tipperary 4-24, Antrim 3-9

1990:   Cork 5-15, Galway 2-21

1991:   Tipperary 1-16, Kilkenny 0-15

1992:   Kilkenny 3-10, Cork 1-12

1993:   Kilkenny 2-17, Galway 1-15

1994:   Offaly 3-16, Limerick 2-13

1995:   Clare 1-13, Offaly 2-8

1996:   Wexford 1-13, Limerick 0-14

1997:   Clare 0-20, Tipperary 2-13
1998:   Offaly 2-16, Kilkenny 1-13
1999:   Cork 0-13, Kilkenny 0-12
2000:   Kilkenny 5-15, Offaly 1-14
2001:   Tipperary 2-18, Galway 2-15
2002:   Kilkenny 2-20, Clare 0-19
2003:   Kilkenny 1-14, Cork 1-11
2004:   Cork 0-17, Kilkenny 0-9
2005:   Cork 1-21, Galway 1-16
2006:   Kilkenny 1-16, Cork 1-13
2007:   Kilkenny 2-19, Limerick 1-15
2008:   Kilkenny 3-30, Waterford 1-13

ALL-IRELAND MINOR HURLING WINNERS

1928:   Cork 1-8, Dublin 3-2 (Draw)
Replay: Cork 7-6, Dublin 0-4
1929:   Waterford 5-0, Meath 1-1
1930:   Tipperary 4-1, Kilkenny 2-1
1931:   Kilkenny 4-7, Galway 2-3
1932:   Tipperary 8-6, Kilkenny 5-1
1933:   Tipperary 4-6, Galway 2-3
1934:   Tipperary 4-3, Laois 3-5
1935:   Kilkenny 4-2, Tipperary 3-3
1936:   Kilkenny 2-4, Cork 2-3
1937:   Cork 8-5, Kilkenny 2-7
1938:   Cork 7-2, Dublin 5-4
1939:   Cork 5-2, Kilkenny 2-2

Facts and Figures

1940:   Limerick 6-4, Antrim 2-4

1941:   Cork 3-11, Galway 1-1

1942–44: No championship held

1945:   Dublin 3-14, Tipperary 4-6

1946:   Dublin 1-6, Tipperary 0-7

1947:   Tipperary 9-5, Galway 1-5

1948:   Waterford 3-8, Kilkenny 4-2

1949:   Tipperary 6-5, Kilkenny 2-4

1950:   Kilkenny 3-4, Tipperary 1-5

1951:   Cork 4-5, Galway 1-8

1952:   Tipperary 9-9, Dublin 2-3

1953:   Tipperary 8-6, Dublin 3-6

1954:   Dublin 2-7, Tipperary 2-3

1955:   Tipperary 5-15, Galway 2-5

1956:   Tipperary 4-16, Kilkenny 1-5

1957:   Tipperary 4-6, Kilkenny 3-7

1958:   Limerick 5-8, Galway 3-10

1959:   Tipperary 2-8, Kilkenny 2-7

1960:   Kilkenny 7-12, Tipperary 1-11

1961:   Kilkenny 3-13, Tipperary 0-15

1962:   Kilkenny 3-6, Tipperary 0-9

1963:   Wexford 6-12, Limerick 5-9

1964:   Cork 10-7, Laois 1-4

1965:   Dublin 4-10, Limerick 2-7

1966:   Wexford 6-7, Cork 6-7 (Draw)

Replay: Wexford 4-1, Cork 1-8

1967:   Cork 2-15, Waterford 5-3

1968:   Wexford 2-13, Cork 3-7

1969:   Cork 2-15, Kilkenny 3-6

1970:   Cork 5-19, Galway 2-9

1971:   Cork 2-11, Kilkenny 1-11

1972:   Kilkenny 8-7, Cork 3-9
1973:   Kilkenny 4-5, Galway 3-7
1974:   Cork 1-10, Kilkenny 1-8
1975:   Kilkenny 3-19, Cork 1-14
1976:   Tipperary 2-20, Kilkenny 1-7
1977:   Kilkenny 4-8, Cork 3-11 (Draw)
Replay: Kilkenny 1-8, Cork 0-9
1978:   Cork 1-15, Kilkenny 1-8
1979:   Cork 2-11, Kilkenny 1-9
1980:   Tipperary 2-15, Wexford 1-10
1981:   Kilkenny 1-20, Galway 3-9
1982:   Tipperary 2-7, Galway 0-4
1983:   Galway 0-10, Dublin 0-7
1984:   Limerick 1-14, Kilkenny 3-8 (Draw)
Replay: Limerick 2-5, Kilkenny 2-4
1985:   Cork 3-10, Wexford 0-12
1986:   Offaly 3-12, Cork 3-9
1987:   Offaly 2-8, Tipperary 0-12
1988:   Kilkenny 3-13, Cork 0-12
1989:   Offaly 2-16, Clare 1-12
1990:   Kilkenny 3-14, Cork 3-14 (Draw)
Replay: Kilkenny 3-16, Cork 0-11
1991:   Kilkenny 0-15, Tipperary 1-10
1992:   Galway 1-13, Waterford 2-4
1993:   Kilkenny 1-17, Galway 1-12
1994:   Galway 2-10, Cork 1-11
1995:   Cork 2-10, Kilkenny 1-2
1996:   Tipperary 3-11, Galway 0-20 (Draw)
Replay: Tipperary 2-14, Galway 2-12
1997:   Clare 1-11, Galway 1-9
1998:   Cork 2-15, Kilkenny 1-9

Facts and Figures

1999:   Galway 0-13, Tipperary 0-10

2000:   Galway 2-19, Cork 4-10

2001:   Cork 2-10, Galway 1-8

2002:   Kilkenny 3-15, Tipperary 1-7

2003:   Kilkenny 2-16, Galway 2-15

2004:   Galway 3-12, Kilkenny 1-18 (Draw)

Replay: Galway 0-16, Kilkenny 1-12

2005:   Galway 3-12, Limerick 0-17

2006:   Tipperary 2-18, Galway 2-7

2007:   Tipperary 3-14, Cork 2-11

2008:   Kilkenny 3-06, Galway 0-13

ALL-IRELAND HURLING CLUB WINNERS

1971:   Roscrea (Tipperary) 4-5, St Rynagh's (Offaly) 2-5

1972:   Blackrock (Cork) 5-13, Rathnure (Wexford) 6-9

1973:   Glen Rovers (Cork) 2-18, St Rynagh's (Offaly) 2-8

1974:   Blackrock (Cork) 3-8, Rathnure (Wexford) 1-9

1975:   St Finbarr's (Cork) Fenians (Kilkenny) 1-6

1976:   James Stephens (Kilkenny) 2-10, Blackrock (Cork) 2-4

1977:   Glen Rovers (Cork) 2-12, Camross (Laois) 0-8

1978:   St Finbarr's (Cork) 2-7, Rathnure (Wexford) 0-9

1979:   Blackrock (Cork) 5-7, Ballyhale Shamrocks (Kilkenny) 5-5

1980:   Castlegar (Galway) 1-11, Ballycastle (Antrim) 1-8

1981:   Ballyhale Shamrocks (Kilkenny) 1-15, St Finbarr's (Cork) 1-11

1982:   James Stephens (Kilkenny) 3-13, Mount Sion (Waterford) 3-8

1983:   Loughgiel Shamrocks (Antrim) 1-8, St Rynagh's (Offaly) 2-5 (Draw)

Replay: Loughgiel Shamrocks 2-12, St Rynagh's 1-12

1984:   Ballyhale Shamrocks (Kilkenny) 1-10, Gort (Galway) 1-10 (Draw)

Replay: Ballyhale Shamrocks 1-10, Gort 0-7

1985: St Martin's (Kilkenny) 2-9, Castlegar (Galway 3-6 (Draw)

Replay: St Martin's 1-13, Castlegar 1-10

1986: Kilruane McDonagh's (Tipperary) 1-15, Buffer's Alley (Wexford) 2-10

1987: Borrisoleigh (Tipperary) 2-9, Rathnure (Wexford) 0-9

1988: Midleton (Cork) 3-8, Athenry (Galway) 0-9

1989: Buffer's Alley (Wexford) 2-12, O'Donovan Rossa (Antrim) 0-12

1990: Ballyhale Shamrocks (Kilkenny) 1-16, Ballybrown (Limerick) 0-16

1991: Glenmore (Kilkenny) 1-13, Patrickswell (Limerick) 0-12

1992: Kiltomer (Galway) 0-15, Birr (Offaly) 1-8

1993: Sarsfields (Galway) 1-17, Kilmallock (Limerick) 2-7

1994: Sarsfields (Galway) 1-14, Toomevara (Tipperary) 3-6

1995: Birr (Offaly) 0-9, Dunloy (Antrim) 0-9 (Draw)

Replay: Birr 3-13, Dunloy 2-3

1996: Sixmilebridge (Clare) 5-10, Dunloy (Antrim) 2-8

1997: Athenry (Galway) 0-14, Wolfe Tones (Clare) 1-8

1998: Birr (Offaly) 1-13, Sarsfields (Galway) 0-9

1999: St Joseph's, Doora-Barefield (Clare) 2-14, Rathnure (Wexford) 0-8

2000: Athenry (Galway) 0-16, St Joseph's, Doora-Barefield (Clare) 0-12

2001: Athenry (Galway) 3-24, Graigue-Ballycallan (Kilkenny) 2-19

2002: Birr (Offaly) 2-10, Clarinbridge (Galway) 1-5

2003: Birr (Offaly) 1-19, Dunloy (Antrim) 0-11

2004: Newtownshandrum (Cork) 0-17, Dunloy (Antrim) 1-6

2005: James Stephens (Kilkenny) 0-19, Athenry (Galway) 0-14

2006: Portumna (Galway) 2-8, Newtownshandrum (Cork) 1-6

2007: Ballyhale Shamrocks (Kilkenny) 3-12, Loughrea (Galway) 2-8

2008: Portumna (Galway) 3-19, Birr (Offaly) 3-9

HURLING TITLES HELD

All-Ireland Senior Titles

31: Kilkenny – 1904, 1905, 1907, 1909, 1911, 1912, 1913, 1922, 1932, 1933, 1935, 1939, 1947, 1957, 1963, 1967, 1969, 1972, 1974, 1975, 1979, 1982, 1983, 1992, 1993, 2000, 2002, 2003, 2006, 2007, 2008

30: Cork – 1890, 1892, 1893, 1894, 1902, 1903, 1919, 1926, 1928, 1929, 1931, 1941, 1942, 1943, 1944, 1946, 1952, 1953, 1954, 1966, 1970, 1976, 1977, 1978, 1984, 1986, 1990, 1999, 2004, 2005

25: Tipperary – 1887, 1895, 1896, 1898, 1899, 1900, 1906, 1908, 1916, 1925, 1930, 1937, 1945, 1949, 1950, 1951, 1958, 1961, 1962, 1964, 1965, 1971, 1989, 1991, 2001

7: Limerick – 1897, 1918, 1921, 1934, 1936, 1940, 1973

6: Dublin – 1889, 1917, 1920, 1924, 1927, 1938

6: Wexford – 1910, 1955, 1956, 1960, 1968, 1996

4: Galway – 1923, 1980, 1987, 1988

4: Offaly – 1981, 1985, 1994, 1998

3: Clare – 1914, 1995, 1997

2: Waterford – 1948, 1959

1: Kerry – 1891

1: Laois – 1915

1: London – 1901

All-Ireland Minor Hurling Titles

19: Kilkenny – 1931, 1935, 1936, 1950, 1960, 1961, 1962, 1972, 1973, 1975, 1977, 1981, 1988, 1990, 1991, 1993, 2002, 2003, 2008

18: Cork – 1928, 1937, 1938, 1939, 1941, 1951, 1964, 1967, 1969, 1970, 1971, 1974, 1978, 1979, 1985, 1995, 1998, 2001

18: Tipperary - 1930, 1932, 1933, 1934, 1947, 1949 1952, 1953, 1955, 1956, 1957, 1959, 1976, 1980, 1982, 1996, 2006, 2007

7: Galway – 1983, 1992, 1994, 1999, 2000, 2004, 2005

4: Dublin – 1945, 1946, 1954, 1965

3: Limerick – 1940, 1958, 1984

3: Offaly – 1986, 1987, 1989

3: Wexford – 1963, 1958, 1968

2: Waterford – 1929, 1948

1: Clare – 1997

All-Ireland U-21 Hurling Titles

11: Cork – 1966, 1968, 1969, 1970, 1971, 1973, 1976, 1982, 1988, 1997, 1998

11: Kilkenny – 1974, 1975, 1977, 1984, 1990, 1994, 1999, 2002, 2004, 2006, 2008

9: Galway – 1972, 1978, 1983, 1986, 1991, 1993, 1996, 2005, 2007

8: Tipperary – 1964, 1967, 1979, 1980, 1981, 1985, 1989, 1995

4: Limerick – 1987, 2000, 2001, 2002

1: Waterford – 1992

1: Wexford – 1965

National Hurling League Titles

19: Tipperary – 1928, 1949, 1950, 1952, 1954, 1955, 1957, 1959,

Facts and Figures

1960, 1961, 1964, 1965, 1968, 1979, 1988, 1994, 1999, 2001, 2008

14: Cork – 1926, 1930, 1940, 1941, 1948, 1953, 1969, 1970, 1972, 1974, 1980, 1981, 1993, 1998

13: Kilkenny – 1933, 1962, 1966, 1976, 1982, 1983, 1986, 1990, 1995, 2002, 2003, 2005, 2006

11: Limerick – 1934, 1935, 1936, 1937, 1938, 1947, 1971, 1984, 1985, 1992, 1997

8: Galway – 1932, 1951, 1975, 1987, 1989, 1996, 2000, 2004

4: Wexford – 1956, 1958, 1967, 1973

3: Clare – 1946, 1977, 1978

2: Dublin – 1929, 1939

2: Waterford – 1963, 2007

1: Offaly – 1991

Railway Cup Titles

44: Munster - 1928, 1929, 1930, 1931, 1934, 1935, 1937, 1938, 1939, 1940, 1942, 1943, 1944, 1945, 1946, 1948, 1949, 1950, 1951, 1952, 1953, 1955, 1957, 1958, 1959, 1960, 1961, 1963, 1966, 1968, 1969, 1970, 1976, 1978, 1981, 1984, 1985, 1992, 1995, 1996, 1997, 2000, 2001, 2005, 2007

24: Leinster – 1927, 1932, 1933, 1936, 1941, 1954, 1956, 1962, 1964, 1965, 1967, 1971, 1972, 1973, 1974, 1975, 1977, 1979, 1988, 1993, 1998, 1999, 2002, 2003, 2006

11: Connacht – 1947, 1980, 1982, 1983, 1986, 1987, 1989, 1991, 1994, 1999, 2004

ALL-IRELAND SENIOR FOOTBALL WINNERS

1887:   Limerick 1-4, Louth 0-3

1888:   No championship

1889:   Tipperary 2-6, Laois 0-0

1890:   Cork 2-4, Wexford 0-1

1891:   Dublin 2-1, Cork 1-9* (Goal worth more than any number of points.)

1892:   Dublin 1-4, Kerry 0-3

1893:   Wexford 1-1, Cork 0-1

1894:   Dublin 0-6, Cork 1-1 (Goals now valued at 5 points) Game drawn.

Replay: Game abandoned with Cork leading 1-2 to 0-5. Match awarded to Dublin.

1895:   Tipperary 0-4, Meath 0-3

1896:   Limerick 1-5, Dublin 0-7 (Goals now valued at 3 points.)

1897:   Dublin 2-6, Cork 0-2

1898:   Dublin 2-8, Waterford 0-4

1899:   Dublin 1-10, Cork 0-6

1900:   Tipperary 3-7, London 0-2

1901:   Dublin 0-14, London 0-2

1902:   Dublin 2-8, London 0-4

1903:   Kerry 0-11, London 0-3

1904:   Kerry 0-5, Dublin 0-2

1905:   Kildare 1-7, Kerry 0-5

1906:   Dublin 0-5, Cork 0-4

1907:   Dublin 0-6, Cork 0-2

1908:   Dublin 1-10, London 0-4

Facts and Figures

1909:   Kerry 1-9, Louth 0-5
1910:   Louth declared winners after Kerry refused to travel to final
1911:   Cork 6-6, Antrim 1-2
1912:   Louth 1-7, Antrim 1-2
1913:   Kerry 2-2, Wexford 0-3
1914:   Kerry 1-3, Wexford 2-0 (Draw)
Replay: Kerry 2-3, Wexford 0-6
1915:   Wexford 2-4, Kerry 2-1
1916:   Wexford 3-4, Mayo 1-2
1917:   Wexford 0-9, Clare 0-5
1918:   Wexford 0-5, Tipperary 0-4
1919:   Kildare 2-5, Galway 0-1
1920:   Tipperary 1-6, Dublin 1-2
1921:   Dublin 1-9, Mayo 0-2
1922:   Dublin 0-6, Galway 0-4
1923:   Dublin 1-5, Kerry 1-3
1924:   Kerry 0-4, Dublin 0-3
1925:   Galway declared winners
1926:   Kerry 1-3, Kildare 0-6 (Draw)
Replay: Kerry 1-4, Kildare 0-4
1927:   Kildare 0-5, Kerry 0-3
1928:   Kildare 2-5, Cavan 2-5
1929:   Kerry 1-8, Kildare 1-5
1930:   Kerry 3-11, Monaghan 1-2
1931:   Kerry 1-11, Kildare 0-8
1932:   Kerry 2-7, Mayo 2-4
1933:   Cavan 2-5, Galway 1-4
1934:   Galway 3-5, Dublin 1-9
1935:   Cavan 3-6, Kildare 2-5
1936:   Mayo 4-11, Laois 0-5
1937:   Kerry 2-5, Cavan 1-8 (Draw)

Replay: Kerry 4-4, Cavan 1-7

1938:   Galway 3-3, Kerry 2-6 (Draw)

Replay: Galway 2-4, Kerry 0-7

1939:   Kerry 2-5, Meath 2-3

1940:   Kerry 0-7, Galway 1-3

1941:   Kerry 1-8, Galway 0-7

1942:   Dublin 1-10, Galway 1-8

1943:   Roscommon 1-6, Cavan 1-6 (Draw)

Replay: Roscommon 2-7, Cavan 2-2

1944:   Roscommon 1-9, Kerry 2-4

1945:   Cork 2-5, Cavan 0-7

1946:   Kerry 2-4, Roscommon 1-7 (Draw)

Replay: Kerry 2-8, Roscommon 0-10

1947:   Cavan 2-11, Kerry 2-7

1948:   Cavan 4-5, Mayo 4-4

1949:   Meath 1-10, Cavan 1-6

1950:   Mayo 2-5, Louth 1-6

1951:   Mayo 2-8, Meath 0-9

1952:   Cavan 2-4, Meath 0-7 (Draw)

Replay: Cavan 0-9, Meath 0-5

1953:   Kerry 0-13, Armagh 1-6

1954:   Meath 1-13, Kerry 1-7

1955:   Kerry 0-12, Dublin 1-6

1956:   Galway 2-13, Cork 3-7

1957:   Louth 1-9, Cork 1-7

1958:   Dublin 2-12, Derry 1-9

1959:   Kerry 3-7, Galway 1-4

1960:   Down 2-10, Kerry 0-8

1961:   Down 3-6, Offaly 2-8

1962:   Kerry 1-12, Roscommon 1-6

1963:   Dublin 1-9, Galway 0-10

Facts and Figures

1964:   Galway 0-15, Kerry 0-10

1965:   Galway 0-12, Kerry 0-9

1966:   Galway 1-10, Meath 0-7

1967:   Meath 1-9, Cork 0-9

1968:   Down 2-12, Kerry 0-13

1969:   Kerry 0-10, Offaly 0-7

1970:   Kerry 2-19, Meath 0-18

1971:   Offaly 1-14, Galway 2-8

1972:   Offaly 1-13, Kerry 1-13 (Draw)

Replay: Offaly 1-19, Kerry 0-13

1973:   Cork 3-17, Galway 2-13

1974:   Dublin 0-14, Galway 1-6

1975:   Kerry 2-12, Dublin 0-11

1976:   Dublin 3-8, Kerry 0-10

1977:   Dublin 5-12, Armagh 3-6

1978:   Kerry 5-11, Dublin 0-9

1979:   Kerry 3-13, Dublin 1-8

1980:   Kerry 1-9, Roscommon 1-6

1981:   Kerry 1-12, Offaly 0-8

1982:   Offaly 1-15, Kerry 0-17

1983:   Dublin 1-10, Galway 1-8

1984:   Kerry 0-14, Dublin 1-6

1985:   Kerry 2-12, Dublin 2-8

1986:   Kerry 2-15, Tyrone 1-10

1987:   Meath 1-14, Cork 0-11

1988:   Meath 0-12, Cork 1-9 (Draw)

Replay: Meath 0-13, Cork 0-12

1989:   Cork 0-17, Mayo 1-11

1990:   Cork 0-11, Meath 0-9

1991:   Down 1-16, Meath 1-14

1992:   Donegal 0-18, Dublin 0-14

1993: Derry 1-14, Cork 2-8
1994: Down 1-12, Dublin 0-13
1995: Dublin 1-10, Tyrone 0-12
1996: Meath 0-12, Mayo 1-9 (Draw)
Replay: Meath 2-9, Mayo 1-11
1997: Kerry 0-13, Mayo 1-7
1998: Galway 1-14, Kildare 1-10
1999: Meath 1-11, Cork 1-8
2000: Kerry 0-14, Galway 0-14 (Draw)
Replay: Kerry 0-17, Galway 1-10
2001: Galway 0-17, Meath 0-8
2002: Armagh 1-12, Kerry 0-14
2003: Tyrone 0-12, Armagh 0-9
2004: Kerry 1-20, Mayo 2-9
2005: Tyrone 1-16, Kerry 2-10
2006: Kerry 4-15, Mayo 3-5
2007: Kerry 3-13, Cork 1-9
2008: Tyrone 1-15, Kerry 0-14

ALL-IRELAND MINOR FOOTBALL WINNERS

1929: Clare 5-3, Longford 3-5
1930: Dublin 1-3, Mayo 0-5
1931: Kerry 3-4, Louth 0-4
1932: Kerry 3-8, Laois 1-3
1933: Kerry 4-1, Mayo 0-9
1934: Tipperary declared winners
1935: Mayo 1-6, Tipperary 1-1
1936: Louth 5-1, Kerry 1-8
1937: Cavan 1-11, Wexford 1-5
1938: Cavan 3-3, Kerry 0-8

Facts and Figures

1939:	Roscommon 1-9, Monaghan 1-7
1940:	Louth 5-5, Mayo 2-7
1941:	Roscommon 3-6, Louth 0-7
1942–44:	No championship played
1945:	Dublin 4-7, Leitrim 0-4
1946:	Kerry 3-7, Dublin 2-3
1947:	Tyrone 4-4, Mayo 4-3
1948:	Tyrone 0-11, Dublin 1-5
1949:	Armagh 1-7, Kerry 1-5
1950:	Kerry 3-6, Wexford 1-4
1951:	Roscommon 2-7, Armagh 1-5
1952:	Galway 2-9, Cavan 1-6
1953:	Mayo 2-11, Clare 1-6
1954:	Dublin 3-3, Kerry 1-8
1955:	Dublin 5-4, Tipperary 2-7
1956:	Dublin 5-14, Leitrim 2-2
1957:	Meath 3-9, Armagh 0-4
1958:	Dublin 2-10, Mayo 0-8
1959:	Dublin 0-11, Cavan 1-4
1960:	Galway 4-9, Cork 1-5
1961:	Cork 3-7, Mayo 0-5
1962:	Kerry 6-5, Mayo 0-7
1963:	Kerry 1-10, Westmeath 0-2
1964:	Offaly 0-15, Cork 1-11
1965:	Derry 2-8, Kerry 2-4
1966:	Mayo 1-12, Down 1-8
1967:	Cork 5-14, Laois 2-3
1968:	Cork 3-5, Sligo 1-10
1969:	Cork 2-7, Derry 0-11
1970:	Galway 1-8, Kerry 2-5 (Draw)
Replay:	Galway 1-11, Kerry 1-10

1971: Mayo 2-15, Cork 2-7
1972: Cork 3-11, Tyrone 2-11
1973: Tyrone 2-11, Kildare 1-6
1974: Cork 1-10, Mayo 1-6
1975: Kerry 1-10, Tyrone 0-4
1976: Galway 1-10, Cork 0-6
1977: Down 2-6, Meath 0-4
1978: Mayo 4-9, Dublin 3-8
1979: Dublin 0-10, Kerry 1-6
1980: Kerry 3-12, Derry 0-11
1981: Cork 4-9, Derry 2-7
1982: Dublin 1-11, Kerry 1-5
1983: Derry 0-8, Cork 1-3
1984: Dublin 1-9, Tipperary 0-4
1985: Mayo 3-3, Cork 0-9
1986: Galway 3-8, Cork 2-7
1987: Down 1-12, Cork 1-5
1988: Kerry 2-5, Dublin 0-5
1989: Derry 3-9, Offaly 1-6
1990: Meath 2-11, Kerry 1-9
1991: Cork 1-9, Mayo 1-7
1992: Meath 2-5, Armagh 0-10
1993: Cork 2-7, Meath 0-9
1994: Kerry 0-16, Galway 1-7
1995: Westmeath 1-10, Derry 0-11
1996: Laois 2-11, Kerry 1-11
1997: Laois 3-11, Tyrone 1-14
1998: Tyrone 2-11, Laois 0-11
1999: Down 1-14, Mayo 0-14
2000: Cork 2-12, Mayo 0-13
2001: Tyrone 0-15, Dublin 1-12 (Draw)

Facts and Figures

Replay: Tyrone 2-11, Dublin 0-6
2002: Derry 1-12, Meath 0-8
2003: Laois 1-11, Dublin 1-11 (Draw)
Replay: Laois 2-10, Dublin 1-9
2004: Tyrone 0-12, Kerry 0-10
2005: Down 1-15, Mayo 0-8
2006: Roscommon 0-15, Kerry 0-15 (Draw)
Replay: Roscommon 1-10, Kerry 0-9
2007: Galway 1-10, Derry 1-9
2008: Tyrone 0-14, Mayo 0-14 (Draw)
Replay: Tyrone 1-20, Mayo 1-15

ALL-IRELAND FOOTBALL CLUB WINNERS

1971: East Kerry (Kerry) 5-9, Bryansford (Down) 2-7
1972: Bellaghy (Derry) 0-15, UCC (Cork) 1-11
1973: Nemo Rangers (Cork) 2-11, St Vincent's (Dublin) 2-11 (Draw)
Replay: Nemo Rangers 4-6, St Vincent's 0-10
1974: UCD (Dublin) 1-6, Clan na Gael (Armagh) 1-6 (Draw)
Replay: UCD 0-14, Clan na Gael 1-4
1975: UCD (Dublin) 1-11, Nemo Rangers (Cork) 0-12
1976: St Vincent's (Dublin) 4-10, Roscommon Gaels (Roscommon) 0-5
1977: Austin Stacks (Kerry) 1-13, Ballerin (Derry) 2-7
1978: Thomond College (Limerick) 2-14, St John's (Belfast) 1-3
1979: Nemo Rangers (Cork) 2-9, Scotstown (Monaghan) 1-3
1980: St Finbarr's (Cork) 3-9, St Grellan's (Galway) 0-8
1981: St Finbarr's (Cork) 1-8, Walterstown (Meath) 0-5
1982: Nemo Rangers (Cork) 6-11, Garrymore (Mayo) 1-8
1983: Portlaoise (Laois) 0-12, Clann na nGael (Roscommon) 2-0

1984:	Nemo Rangers (Cork) 2-10, Walterstown (Meath) 0-5

1984: Nemo Rangers (Cork) 2-10, Walterstown (Meath) 0-5

1985: Castleisland Desmonds (Kerry) 2-2, St Vincent's (Dublin) 0-7

1986: Burren (Down) 1-10, Castleisland Desmonds (Kerry) 1-6

1987: St Finbarr's (Cork) 0-10, Clann na nGael (Roscommon) 0-7

1988: Burren (Down) 1-9, Clann na nGael (Roscommon) 0-8

1989: Nemo Rangers (Cork) 1-13, Clann na nGael (Roscommon) 1-3

1990: Baltinglass (Wicklow) 2-7, Clann na nGael (Roscommon) 0-7

1991: Lavey (Derry) 2-9, Salthill (Galway) 0-10

1992: Dr Crokes (Kerry) 1-11, Thomas Davis (Dublin) 0-13

1993: O'Donovan Rossa (Cork) 1-12, Éire Óg (Carlow) 3-6 (Draw)

Replay: O'Donovan Rossa 1-7, Éire Óg 0-8

1994: Nemo Rangers (Cork) 3-11, Castlebar Mitchels (Mayo) 0-8

1995: Kilmacud Crokes (Dublin) 0-8, Bellaghy (Derry) 0-5

1996: Laune Rangers (Kerry) 4-5, Éire Óg (Carlow) 0-11

1997: Crossmaglen Rangers (Armagh) 2-13, Knockmore (Mayo) 0-11

1998: Corofin (Galway) 0-15, Erin's Isle (Dublin) 0-10

1999: Crossmaglen Rangers (Armagh) 0-9, Ballina Stephenites (Mayo) 0-8

2000: Crossmaglen Rangers (Armagh) 1-14, Na Fianna (Dublin) 0-12

2001: Crossmolina Deel Rovers (Mayo) 0-16, Nemo Rangers (Cork) 0-12

2002: Ballinderry (Derry) 2-10, Nemo Rangers (Cork) 0-9

2003: Nemo Rangers (Cork) 0-14, Crossmolina Deel Rovers (Mayo) 1-9

2004: Caltra (Galway) 0-13, An Ghaeltacht (Kerry) 0-12

2005: Ballina Stephenites (Mayo) 1-12, Portlaoise (Laois) 2-8

2006: Salthill-Knocknacarra (Galway) 0-7, Naomh Gall (Antrim) 0-6

2007: Crossmaglen (Armagh) 0-13, Dr Crokes (Kerry) 1-5

2008: St Vincent's (Dublin) 1-11, Nemo Rangers (Cork) 0-13

FOOTBALL TITLES HELD

All-Ireland Senior Titles:

35: Kerry – 1903, 1904, 1909, 1913, 1914, 1924, 1926, 1929, 1930, 1931, 1932, 1937, 1939, 1940, 1941, 1946, 1953, 1955, 1959, 1962, 1969, 1970, 1975, 1978, 1979, 1980, 1981, 1984, 1985, 1986, 1997, 2000, 2004, 2006, 2007

22: Dublin – 1891, 1892, 1894, 1897, 1898, 1899, 1901, 1902, 1906, 1907, 1908, 1921, 1922, 1923,1942, 1958, 1963, 1974, 1976, 1977, 1983, 1995

9: Galway – 1925, 1934, 1938, 1956, 1964, 1965, 1966, 1998, 2001

7: Meath – 1949, 1954, 1967, 1987, 1988, 1996, 1999

6: Cork – 1890, 1911, 1945, 1973, 1989, 1990

5: Wexford – 1893, 1915, 1916, 1917, 1918

5: Cavan – 1933, 1935, 1947, 1948, 1952

5: Down – 1960, 1961, 1968, 1991, 1994

4: Kildare: 1905, 1919, 1927, 1928

4: Tipperary – 1889, 1895, 1900, 1920

3: Louth – 1910, 1912, 1957

3: Mayo – 1936, 1950, 1951

3: Offaly – 1971, 1972, 1982

3: Tyrone – 2003, 2005, 2008

2: Limerick – 1887, 1896

2: Roscommon – 1943, 1944

1: Donegal – 1992

1: Derry – 1993

1: Armagh – 2002

All-Ireland Minor Titles:

11: Kerry – 1931, 1932, 1933, 1946, 1950, 1962, 1963, 1975, 1980, 1988, 1994

10: Cork – 1961, 1967, 1968, 1969, 1972, 1974, 1980, 1991, 1993, 2000

10: Dublin – 1930, 1945, 1954, 1955, 1956, 1958, 1959, 1979, 1982, 1984

7: Tyrone – 1947, 1948, 1973, 1998, 2001, 2004, 2008

6: Mayo – 1935, 1953, 1966, 1971, 1978, 1985

5: Galway – 1952, 1960, 1970, 1976, 1986, 2007

4: Derry – 1965, 1983, 1989, 2002

4: Roscommon – 1939, 1941, 1951, 2006

4: Down – 1977, 1987, 1999, 2005

3: Meath – 1957, 1990, 1992

3: Laois – 1996, 1997, 2003

2: Cavan – 1937, 1938

2: Louth - 1936, 1940

1: Armagh – 1949

1: Clare – 1929

1: Offaly – 1964

1: Tipperary – 1935

1: Westmeath – 1995

All-Ireland U-21 Titles:

10: Cork – 1970, 1971, 1980, 1981, 1984, 1985, 1986, 1989, 1994, 2007

10: Kerry – 1964, 1973, 1975, 1976, 1977, 1990, 1995, 1996, 1998, 2008

4: Mayo – 1967, 1974, 1983, 2006

4: Tyrone – 1991, 1992, 2000, 2001

3: Galway – 1972, 2002, 2005

2: Derry – 1968, 1997

2: Donegal – 1982, 1987

Facts and Figures

2: Roscommon – 1966, 1978
1: Antrim – 1969
1: Armagh – 2004
1: Down – 1979
1: Dublin – 2003
1: Kildare – 1965
1: Meath – 1993
1: Offaly – 1998
1: Westmeath – 1999

National Football League Titles

18: Kerry – 1928, 1929, 1931, 1932, 1959, 1961, 1963, 1969, 1971, 1972, 1973, 1974, 1977, 1982, 1984, 1997, 2004, 2006
11: Mayo – 1934, 1935, 1936, 1937, 1938, 1939, 1941, 1949, 1954, 1970, 2001
8: Dublin – 1953, 1955, 1958, 1976, 1978, 1987, 1991, 1993
7: Meath – 1933, 1946, 1951, 1975, 1988, 1990, 1994
6: Derry – 1947, 1992, 1995, 1996, 2000, 2008
4: Cork – 1952, 1956, 1980, 1989
4: Down – 1960, 1962, 1968, 1983
4: Galway – 1940, 1957, 1965, 1981
3: New York – 1950, 1964, 1967
2: Laois – 1927, 1986
2: Tyrone – 2002, 2003
1: Cavan – 1948
1: Longford – 1966
1: Monaghan – 1985
1: Offaly – 1998
1: Roscommon – 1979
1: Armagh – 2005
1: Donegal – 2007

Railway Cup Titles

28: Leinster – 1928, 1929, 1930, 1932, 1933, 1935, 1939, 1940, 1944, 1945, 1952, 1953, 1954, 1955, 1959, 1961, 1962, 1974, 1985, 1986, 1987, 1988, 1996, 1997, 2000, 2002, 2005, 2006

27: Ulster – 1942, 1943, 1947, 1950, 1956, 1960, 1963, 1964, 1965, 1966, 1968, 1970, 1971, 1979, 1980, 1983, 1984, 1989, 1991, 1992, 1993, 1994, 1995, 1998, 2000, 2003, 2004, 2007

14: Munster – 1927, 1931, 1941, 1946, 1948, 1949, 1972, 1975, 1976, 1977, 1978, 1981, 1982, 1999

9: Connacht – 1934, 1936, 1937, 1938, 1951, 1957, 1958, 1967, 1969

1: Combined Universities – 1973

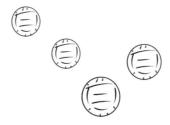